Louis XIV

P.A. Holmes

Series Editors
Michael and Mollie Hardwick

Evergreen Lives

ISBN 0 7127 0004 8

Series Editors
Michael and Mollie Hardwick

Design by Roy Lee

Production by Bob Towell

Colour Separations
by
D.S. Colour International Limited, London
Photo-typesetting
by
Sayers Clark Limited, Croydon, Surrey

Printed and bound in Spain by
TONSA, San Sebastian

Contents

Select Bibliography

MAURICE ASHLEY - *Louis the XIV and the Greatness of France* (New York 1965)

WILLIAM F. CHURCH - *The Greatness of Louis XIV - Myth or Reality?* (Boston 1959)

VINCENT CRONIN - *Louis XIV* (London 1965)

PHILIPPE ERLANGER - *Louis XIV* (London 1970)

RAGNHILD HATTON - *Louis XIV and his world* (London 1972)

CHRISTOPHER HIBBERT - *Versailles* (New York 1972)

ALVA GONZALES PALACIOS - *The Age of Louis XIV* (London 1969)

NANCY MITFORD - *The Sun King* (New York 1966)

JOANNA RICHARDSON - *Louis XIV* (London 1973)

Chronology

1638   5 September, Louis born in the Château of Saint-Germain-en-Laye outside Paris.

1642   Death of Cardinal Richelieu on 4 December.

1643   Death of Louis XIII on 14 May. Mazarin made Prime Minister.

1648   Outbreak of civil wars known as the *Fronde*.

1651   7 September, Louis assumes government at 13.

1652   End of the *Fronde*.

1654   Louis crowned in Rheims Cathedral, 7 June.

1660   Louis marries Marie-Thérèse, daughter of Philip IV of Spain, 9 June.

1661   Death of Mazarin, 9 March. Fouquet arrested. Louis takes command of the Army. Louise de la Vallière becomes his mistress.

1665   Death of King Philip IV of Spain. Colbert replaces Mazarin.

1667   War of the Spanish Devolution.

1668   Athénaïs de Montespan replaces La Vallière.

1678 Treaty of Nijmegen ends Dutch war.

1682 The Court moves to Versailles.

1683 Death of Queen Marie-Thérèse. Secret marriage of Louis and Madame de Maintenon.

1686 Formation of League of Augsburg, against France.

1688 France invades Western Germany.

1697 Treaty of Ryswick ends the war.

1700 Death of Charles II of Spain. Philippe V, grandson of Louis, proclaimed King of Spain.

1701 Formation of Grand Alliance against France. Death of the King's brother Philippe ('Monsieur'). War of Spanish Succession.

1704 French defeat at the Battle of Blenheim.

1706 11 May, Marlborough victor at Ramillies.

1709 Widespread famine in France in severe winter. Marlborough victor at Malplaquet.

1711 Death of Louis's heir, the Dauphin.

1713 War of Spanish Succession ends.

1715 Death of Louis XIV, 1 September, after the longest reign in European history.

Introduction

'A GREAT COMET' was the description of Louis XIV
by Sir William Temple, British Ambassador to the
Hague, a man who was on the spot to observe the
dazzling progress of that comet across the skies of
the seventeenth century. A caricaturist might well
have drawn Louis as such, arrogant nose and chin
jutting prowlike, long abundant ringlets streaming
behind him, light flashing from his ceremonial
armour and surrounding him with the golden aura
of absolute kingship. For what, by definition, is a
comet but a long-haired star?

Born by something like a miracle to parents who
had seemed unable to produce an heir, the name
given to him at his ceremonial baptism was Louis *le
Dieu-Donné*, the God-given. Traditional ideas of
kingship surrounded him from the beginning;
even when he grew too old to have fairy stories read
to him at bedtime, the practice was continued,
substituting an up-to-date History of France which
underlined the virtues of his ancestors, and from
nursery age Louis was encouraged to play at
soldiers in the grandest manner, with a huge army
of silver men, horses and weapons. His mother
adored him; he was the idol of her court. The
brilliant Cardinal Mazarin was his tutor in statecraft; his unbringing was such as could not fail to
produce a great King of France.

All of this heightened the impact of the civil wars
of the *Fronde* upon the privileged child. Suddenly

11

his life of luxury was over. For the first time he knew what insecurity was, as his mother was forced to take him and his small brother away from Paris; but not before mobs had stormed the Palais Royal, demanding to know if the Queen and her sons had already escaped. Louis was sent to bed and told to pretend to be asleep. He managed it convincingly, without flickering an eyelid, conscious of people who had no right to be in his bedchamber filing past, peering in through the drawn-back bed-curtains, staring and talking. It was enough to frighten any ordinary child, but Louis was not ordinary. He was a king, and had been since the age of four. This taste of the revolutionary horrors which were to overtake his decendants during The Terror, a century and more in the future, only strengthened his determination to be absolute ruler. If he never quite forgave the Paris crowds, at least he would make sure that they, his people, would not have to endure civil war again.

There is an allegorical painting of him, seen at the end of the wars of the *Fronde* as a victorious young god, enthroned, robed and armoured like a Roman hero, laurel-crowned, the mask of Anarchy beneath his foot. His expression is mild and amiable; it is not at all characteristic of his feelings. He had been humiliated, had lived in something like poverty, wearing clothes too small for him, but he was not troubled about that. What did trouble him was the poor state of the royal treasury, which he determined to improve; that would be just one thing he would do.

The great Mazarin died when Louis was twenty-three. Often resenting the Cardinal's advice and guidance, he had obeyed, had made the advantageous Spanish marriage to the Infanta Maria Theresa which Mazarin had urged, and had taken note of his mentor's deathbed words: 'Never have a Prime Minister. Govern!' And that was exactly what Louis did, in person, with only a handful of experienced administrators.

He never said *'L'État, c'est moi'*, but the legendary phrase expresses very well the situation he created for himself, ruler of the most powerful and thickly populated nation in Europe, guardian of her military glory, arbiter of taste and manners, patron of the Arts, a law unto himself. Nature had equipped him perfectly for the job. He was handsome, so full of personality that people thought of him as tall, though in fact he was slightly below middle height. He was strong, healthy, athletic, devoted to hunting. His intellectual capacity was limited, but he had a good lively mind and an intense interest in building improvements, architecture and landscape gardening, the theatre and ballet, painting and sculpture. His aims were grand, but not solely for self-aggrandisement. The Duc de Saint-Simon, who disliked him on the whole, said of him that he was 'born with a less than mediocre mind, but a mind capable of moulding, polishing and refining itself, of borrowing from others without imitation and without strain.'

Whatever he may have borrowed, much of what he achieved came from himself alone. Under him, the larger towns of France emerged from the Middle Ages. Paris, whatever her king may have felt about her citizens, benefited enormously. He restored the ancient Cathedral of Notre Dame, completed and enriched the Palais of the Louvre, where much of his childhood had been spent, gave the city the Pont Royal, created the Champs Élysées from swampland, built Les Invalides for old soldiers and the Salpêtriére for the homeless; added two new gates, the Saint-Denis and the Saint-Martin, two great squares, the Place des Victoires and the Place Vendôme. For the first time the dark narrow streets that Villon and his dubious companions had known were illuminated by street-lamps fuelled with whale-oil, fresh drinking-water flowed in new fountains, and houses were built not for moles but for people, with generous windows. The young architect Jules Hardouin Mansart arose to give his name, in a slightly altered form, to the roofs which still characterise French houses.

Of all the things Louis's great energies created, he is best remembered for Versailles, the immense palace he caused to be built on the site of his father's old hunting-lodge, and in 1682 made the seat of monarchy and government, away from plague-infested Paris. It was the most ambitious building ever designed, meant not only to show off the King's wealth and magnificence but to dazzle and humble visiting ambassadors. It stands still, a little changed from the palace Louis knew, and empty of the enormous throng who inhabited it. There is something strange and sad about it, a thing raised to the glory of a man who was only mortal, whatever he may have considered himself to be in the pride of his manhood, when he gave little or no thought to the fact that one day this place would no longer be his home but his monument. Groves and shrubberies, yew-alleys, fountains and marble basins attended by marble children, all testify to the grand design of the king who was more perishable than the smallest artefact in all the mighty Palace of Versailles.

Under Louis's patronage, literature and the Arts soared to new heights. Eminently reasonable (a very fashionable virtue) with a fine feeling for language ('the preciseness of his words is the image of the exactitude of his thoughts', said Bossuet) he drew about him writers who wanted to flatter and please him by reflecting his own tastes in their works. The dramatist Molière made him laugh, was encouraged by him to write satires which a sterner monarch might have banned. The outspoken Boileau was his friend, as was Racine, tragedian, moralist and supreme master of classical drama. In painting, Poussin, Claude Lorrain, Le Brun, Mignard and Rigaud created elaborate, opulent splendour, and inspired many engravers to popularise their work. In architecture, fine houses sprang up, miniature editions of Versailles, in place of decrepit old ones; in music, Lully and Couperin composed with courtly grace and charm music that survives today as freshly as ever. The reign of Louis XIV would leave an indelible mark on the world.

The King's military ambitions had less happy results. 'My dominant passion is certainly love of glory', he said in his memoirs. But *la gloire*, the will-o'-the-wisp which had led him into the long futility of the Dutch wars, was to draw him in the end into the disasters of Blenheim, Malplaquet and Ramillies. A great deal of his beloved France had been lost, with countless numbers of his soldiers, those cheerful *Jolicoeurs* who had once gone into battle singing. It had all been for nothing, in the outcome; he had been wrong, and in bitterness he came to know it. A series of family tragedies, and the terrible Great Frost which paralysed France in 1709, seemed to him the visitation of Heaven. On his deathbed, broken in spirit, he said, 'God punishes me, I have deserved it.'

Those tragedies, caused by such trivial things - a measles germ, a fall from a horse, one bloodletting too many by an ignorant doctor - killed off one by one those who should have been Louis's heirs. Of enormous sexual appetite, he had not succeeded in siring the large family hoped for from his dull dumpy Spanish queen, and even the children of his two principal mistresses, La Vallière and de Montespan, seemed fatally flawed. Whatever sins of arrogance or mistaken idealism Louis committed in his life, in the end he suffered for them; the last descriptions of him show a pathetic figure.

Yet it is the image of Louis in his glory, Louis the Sun King, which history retains. He brought light, grace and grandeur to the country he loved and enriched. Perhaps he has, as one of his biographers has suggested, 'no power over the heart', but in his own time he possessed enormous charm, and, a rarer commodity, surpassing style. Saint-Simon's somewhat inaccurate *Mémoires*, coloured by personal prejudice, reflect Louis unflatteringly, yet now and then a note of reluctant admiration breaks in.

> Never did any man give with better grace, and so increase the value of his favours. Never did man sell his words, his smile, even his glances more splendidly... Never was there one so naturally polite...But, more than all, he was unequalled in his behaviour to women. He would never pass the humblest of bonnets without raising his hat, even to a chambermaid... To the smallest gesture, his

walk, his gait, his whole physiognomy, all was measured, fitting, noble, grand, majestic, and more - very natural.

Grace, courtesy and style may not head the list of qualifications for immortality, but they have been singularly absent from the make-up of many famous people. Louis XIV was not only a great man; he was also a great gentleman.

Michael and Mollie Hardwick

God's Gift to the Nation

1638 – 1647

THE NIGHT SKY ABOVE PARIS glowed with the light from a thousand bonfires, and a sparkling cascade of fireworks burst over a colossal illuminated set-piece depicting the sun rising over a cloud-covered mountain. It was Sunday, 5 September 1638, and the people of France were celebrating the birth of a prince.

'Never has there been such great rejoicing as for this favour that Heaven has granted to the Kingdom of France' announced the Prime Minister, Cardinal Richelieu, as national excitement built up to fever-pitch. Wine flowed from fountains, rich merchants distributed food among the revellers, and religious processions chanting *Te Deums* mingled with the crowds dancing in the streets singing 'Now we have a Dauphin!'

In the Château of Saint-Germain outside Paris, the new baby, a large healthy boy, was washed in wine and oil of red roses, then carried to the palace chapel, where at a simple baptism ceremony he was given his name - Louis. He would later be formally named Louis *le Dieu-Donné*, the God-Given. The arrival of the new prince was certainly considered a miraculous event by the French people, and also by his parents. Louis XIII and his wife, Anne of Austria, daughter of Philip III of Spain, had been married for twenty-three barren years, and hopes of the couple producing an heir to the throne had long since faded.

Married for political reasons when they were both fourteen, the royal pair were distantly related, but it was not a happy match. The young King was quiet and reserved, only really himself when in the hunting field or working with his hands. He would spend hours in his workshops designing and making anything from a gun to a pair of shoes. He was an excellent cook and an accomplished musician. Though not physically strong, he was no coward and had spent many years at the head of his army fighting France's enemies, Spain and Austria. With Cardinal de Richelieu, his principal minister and the driving force behind him, he crushed the Huguenots, followers of the Protestant John Calvin who presented a threat to the established religion of Catholic France, and defended the monarchy from ambitious noblemen and political intrigues.

Women played little part in the King's life. He found himself quite unable to form a satisfactory relationship with the lively Spanish princess who became his wife. Anne was tall and beautiful, with chestnut hair and a fair complexion. Full of vitality, she had a passion for gambling and was a notorious flirt. The prudish Louis was repelled by this exuberant creature; it was nearly three years before he was able to consummate the marriage, and then only after the good-humoured efforts of his relatives and friends teased and coaxed their reluctant monarch to his queen's bed.

After two miscarriages - probably caused because of Anne's habit of romping too boisterously with her ladies - Louis's dislike of the physical side of marriage resulted in his withdrawing further and further from her side. Anne became increasingly immersed in frivolous amusements; it soon became obvious that the royal couple actively disliked one another's company.

As the years passed the question of the Queen's loyalty to France was raised. Cardinal Richelieu was alarmed at the secret correspondence she conducted with her relatives and contacts in Spain, and trapped in a sterile lonely marriage she became involved in a number of political intrigues, as well as a single amorous one with the English Ambassador to Paris, the handsome, dashing Duke of Buckingham. It seems to have been no more than a flirtation on her side, but it gave rise to scandal (and, three centuries later, to Dumas's novel *The Three Musketeers*).

Rumours of divorce alarmed Richelieu, who, alert to the damaging effect the Queen's reputation was having on the monarchy, almost succeeded in persuading the King to send her to a convent. It may have been the realisation of the danger she was in of losing her position and life of pleasure that gradually had a sobering effect on the Queen. She learned to keep her wild behaviour in check, and set out to convince her husband of her loyalty and willingness to please.

The King was aware of the necessity for him to father an heir to the throne if it were at all possible. His brother, Gaston d'Orléans, a weak character and a dangerous man, had been collaborating for many years with the King's enemies; it was well known that he had aspirations to the crown itself.

The awkward situation was resolved by one of those extraordinary accidents which shape history. One late December afternoon in 1637, Louis was returning to one of his country lodges after paying a visit to a convent where he sometimes went to seek advice from Sister Angélique, his ex-mistress now turned nun. Darkness fell. Rain set in, grew heavier, soaking the already rheumatic King and his attendants. Soon it became sleet, falling like hailstones on the shivering train. They were near the Palace of the Louvre; but Louis's apartments in that vast building were unfurnished, quite unready for him. After a great deal of persuasion François de Guitart, captain of the guard, convinced him that as the Queen was in residence at the Louvre the obvious course was to sup and spend the night with her. Louis was far from enthusiastic, but the Queen was delighted to hear of his impending arrival. She did her best to make the evening - and the night - a success.

It was. In March 1638 a happy royal event was predicted. Louis XIV has come down the years to us as the Sun King; more appropriately he might be known as the Rain King.

Louis XIII and Anne of Austria were overjoyed at the birth of their son. The fact that he was born with two teeth was considered an auspicious omen, though one visiting ambassador was heard to comment sourly that it was a portent of the future king's power to 'bite his neighbours' in years to come. The members of the *Parlement* of Paris came to pay their respects, and presents and good wishes poured into the country from foreign kings and princes. Pope Urban VIII sent baby clothes of fine silk embroidered with gold thread to the child he recognised as 'the eldest son of the Church', and the beaded outfit of a Red Indian papoose was sent by the Indians of New France in Canada to 'our Good King'.

Anne was delighted with her son. After so many years of a cold marriage she at last had another human being whom she could love. 'The Queen hardly ever leaves the little Dauphin' it was reported. 'She delights in playing with him and in taking him for drives when the weather is fine. He is her principal pleasure...'

Two years later there was another little prince in the royal nursery. Philippe was named after his maternal grandfather the King of Spain, and given the title Duc d'Anjou. Louis XIII had once given up hope of fathering a future king; now the throne was secure for his family, and even that unemotional man could not disguise his delight. But he was jealous of his children's devotion to their mother. He complained that the Dauphin was shy in the company of adults, and that his mother and the women who surrounded him were encouraging the boy to show hostility towards his father. It was more likely that his own reserved temperament was to blame. As the Dauphin grew older he spent more time in his father's company. If Louis XIII had lived a few years longer it is possible that they would have built up a close relationship. The boy had a great admiration for his father's legendary prowess, both as a soldier and in the hunting field. In spite of failing health the King was still a superb horseman and continued to enjoy the chase and hunt with his falcons, his favourite sport. In his workshop he made with his own hands a miniature arquebus as a present for his son. When he was older the young Louis was to carry it with him as he stalked and shot at sparrows in the Tuileries gardens.

In March 1643 the King's health was deteriorating. He was only forty-two, but in the last stages of tuberculosis. On Maundy Thursday it was the four-year old Dauphin who performed the custom of washing the feet of the poor; but it would be many years before the new King would be mature enough to rule on his own, so there would have to be a Regent. Cardinal Richelieu, the power behind the throne for so many years, had died in the previous December. Louis XIII had to make the greatest decision of his life alone, knowing that the wrong decision could endanger the succession.

He entrusted his wife with the children's education, although he had never completely believed the Spanish-born Queen to have the interests of France at heart. He announced that on his death she should be nominal Regent only, subject to a council of five. 'The Queen must be controlled.' He also named Cardinal Mazarin as godfather to his son, whose formal baptism had been hastily arranged for 21 April.

The Dauphin, so young that he was still in skirts, was taken to the Chapel Royal wearing a long dress of silver taffeta. The Bishop of Meaux anointed him with holy oil and gave him the name that set him apart from all others, Louis *le Dieu-Donné* - Louis the God-Given.

He was taken to his father's bedside after the ceremony.

'What is your name now?' asked the dying King as the child knelt to receive his blessing.

'Louis XIV, Papa,' whispered the boy.

'Not yet, not yet,' his father told him as he kissed him for the last time, 'but it soon will be, if that is God's Will.'

'If my Papa dies I will throw myself into the moat' the weeping child told his attendants. 'I don't want to be King.'

But on 14 May 1643, at the age of four years and eight months, Louis XIV inherited the throne of

France. Next day, dressed in mourning robes of violet velvet, the solemn little figure, very conscious of his new dignity, was taken to Paris in a coach drawn by six white horses.

'*Vive le Roi!*' shouted the people, as the procession moved through streets garlanded with flowers on its way to the Palais de Justice. There was little regret at the passing of the late King. France was looking forward to a new era of peace and prosperity, their hopes centred on the child who appeared before them. A Paris news sheet, *La Gazette*, reported that the new King was 'as beautiful as an angel, displaying in all his actions a modesty and decorum extraordinary in one of his age.'

The small boy with the chestnut curls, a serious expression on his rosy face, was lifted to the throne in front of the two hundred and twenty members of the *Parlement* of Paris. Encouraged by his mother, he recited two sentences: 'Gentlemen, I have come to express my affection and goodwill towards my *Parlement*. My Chancellor will give you my wishes.'

They were not quite his, of course. The Queen had tactfully removed control of the Regency from the hands of the five councillors, and when *Parlement* voted to abolish the Regency council it was announced that the King was graciously pleased to grant his mother 'free, absolute and entire administration' of the kingdom during his minority. Louis XIII had not wanted that; but Louis was dead, laid among his ancestors at Saint-Denis.

The gay, irresponsible young queen of former years had matured into a level-headed woman determined to safeguard her son's heritage and dedicate herself to France. But she knew that she lacked the qualities of an absolute monarch. She turned to the one person on whom she felt she could depend - her son's godfather. On 18 May she named Cardinal Mazarin her Prime Minister.

Jules Mazarin had started life as Giulio Mazzarini. His father had been steward in the household of the powerful Colonna family in Rome, and the Colonnas, recognising the boy's potential, had paid for his education at the Roman College and the University of Alcala. The reputation he had acquired in the Papal diplomatic service had impressed Cardinal Richelieu. When advice or mediation were needed, young Mazarin was there. Richelieu had trained Mazarin as his secretary, and was largely responsible for his rise to power.

Highly cultivated, Mazarin was a connoisseur of the arts, a lover of music, opera and the theatre, and a keen bibliophile. Kindly and unassuming he may have appeared, but his gentle smile and mild exterior concealed a rapier-sharp mind and driving ambition. He had amassed a fortune which allowed him to indulge in his chief pleasures, the building and furnishing of palaces and collecting of works of art and precious stones.

There was great rapport between the still-beautiful Queen of forty-two and the sophisticated cardinal who was the same age. Anne had always had a weakness for an attractive man, and Mazarin, elegant and suave, had much to offer in the way of experience and political contacts. He became indispensable to the Queen, further endearing himself to her by speaking her native tongue when they were together.

Rumours inevitably surrounded the couple, but the Queen was known to have confided to a friend, 'Though my mind is charmed by his mind, my senses are not involved. I admit I like him, but my affection does not amount to love, or if it does it is without my knowledge.' That they ever became lovers is doubtful. It is even less likely that there was a secret marriage, as was long suspected. Mazarin was determined to remain unmarried. Though he had obtained the coveted cardinal's hat through Richelieu's influence he was not an ordained priest. Even so, there was a faint possibility that he could one day stand for election as Pope, to qualify for which it would have been necessary for him to remain celibate. For a man of such ambition, to jeopardise his chances would have been unthinkable.

Mazarin had many enemies, but always insisted that the interests of France were of paramount importance to him. Entrusted with the young

King's upbringing, he was responsible for teaching him statecraft and training him for his position. Louis responded well. 'He has the stuff for several great kings and one good man', his godfather was to write. Mathematics, geography, Spanish, Italian and Latin were taught him by a number of tutors, and his responsibilities as King were continually emphasised. He would be glorious and all-powerful, second only to God: he must always remember this.

'Homage is due to Kings; they act as they please,' he wrote in his copy-book. 'I ought always to remember that I am King so that I do nothing unworthy of my name.'

At the age of seven, Louis officially attained the age of reason. He discarded his dresses for breeches and hose, and was given his own household. He missed the company of his mother and his nurses, and his valet La Porte reported that the King could not sleep without his bedtime fairy stories, his favourite being *Peau d'Âne (Donkey-skin)*, a variation on the Cinderella theme. The Queen was consulted, and it was decided that La Porte should continue the childish custom.

> I said that if her Majesty were agreeable I would read to him out of some good book... I told her that I did not think anything could be more suitable than the history of France, and that I would point out the bad kings to him so he would want to be different from them. The Queen thought it a very good idea... I read to him from Mézéray's History of France every night, as if it were a story, to such effect that the King was pleased, and gave good promise of resembling the nobler of his ancestors, flying into a great rage when it was suggested to him that he might turn out to be a second Louis the Sluggard, for I used to attack his defects quite often, as the Queen had ordered me to do.

Louis was growing into a handsome well-built boy with large hazel eyes and his mother's curly light chestnut hair. He was not a noticeably happy child, rarely laughing even when playing with other children. He was trained by his mother and Mazarin to hide his feelings and curb every impulsive remark, not without reason - there were many dangerous people surrounding him.

There were other children at Court, including Louis's younger brother Philippe. The boys got on well together, opposites as they were - Philippe was a sunny, outgoing, friendly child, who looked like a little girl and behaved rather like one. His mother kept him in petticoats beyond the usual age for being breeched, probably in the hope of preventing him from becoming an active rival to Louis. He grew up bisexual, with a partiality for handsome young men and for dressing like a girl in the company of his depraved young 'mignons'. But he and Louis would always be friends, as they were now, though when they played together it was made clear by Louis that he must be obeyed. He was King and expected to be treated as such. There is a story that when the Prince of Wales, the future Charles II of England, came to visit Louis at Fontainebleau, the two boys played together in complete silence, so conscious was each of his own importance. It seems more likely that the fact that Louis spoke no English and Charles may not have been in the habit of speaking French accounted for their lack of communication.

War games were Louis's greatest pleasure. He would spend hours drilling the older children of the Court, and would march around the grounds leading his retinue, beating excitedly on his drum. However trying the noise, nobody dared complain. Model soldiers made of silver, miniature gold cannon to be drawn by fleas, toy guns which fired blanks and a model fort through which the boys could ride their horses: the King's toys were all designed to encourage his interest in military affairs. But at night-time he was a small boy frightened of the dark, creeping into his valet's bed if he had a nightmare. Every morning before he dressed he was visited by a woman who had been one of his wet-nurses, a carter's wife, Pérette Dufour. She greeted him with a kiss every day, a custom continued

25

whenever possible until her death in 1688, when the King was fifty years old.

In November 1647 the news spread swiftly through France, 'The King's life is despaired of.' Louis had smallpox. For eleven days his life hung in the balance. His enemies gathered to plot how they would seize the crown as soon as his death was confirmed. There was a plan to kidnap the little Philippe; their evil uncle, Gaston d'Orléans, always just in the background when there was trouble, held a supper-party where the guests drank a toast to 'Gaston I, King of France'.

Mazarin's enemies in the Paris *Parlement* seized on the opportunity to plan to get rid of him as soon as a new Regency could be declared. No more foreigners would have the opportunity to run France, particularly 'that Italian monkey'.

But the King recovered, in spite of the doctors' bleeding and purging. Anne of Austria and Cardinal Mazarin were still in power, and Louis XIV sat up in bed and fed his little white pony, which had been brought into his room. A crisis had passed; but Louis's childhood was ending, and there were troubled times ahead.

The Years of the Frondes

1648 – 1652

'GAY, SPRIGHTLY LAND of mirth and social ease' wrote Oliver Goldsmith of seventeenth-century France. But the face that France showed the outside world hid a state of social and political chaos which had afflicted her for decades.

The long religious wars of 1563-1593 between Catholics and Protestant Huguenots had left a legacy of unrest which took years to settle. Henry IV had only been able to bring the wars to an end by issuing the Edict of Nantes in 1598, which gave the Huguenots freedom of worship, the right to hold official posts and to have a private army and garrison a number of fortresses in the kingdom. There were many people who resented Henry's policy of religious toleration, and in 1619 he was murdered by a fanatical Roman Catholic.

Cardinal Richelieu regarded the Huguenots as a threat to the country; as chief minister of France he felt his duty was to destroy their political power. Continually rebelling against Richelieu's policies, they appealed to England for help when they were besieged by French troops in La Rochelle, but in October 1628 the town was captured and its fortifications destroyed. The Huguenots were forced to accept the Peace of Alais, which gave them religious liberty but no political independence.

With the Huguenots crushed, Richelieu concentrated his attentions on the French nobility. If the King, then Louis XIII, was to be the absolute ruler of France, the provincial princes, continually fighting among themselves in their desire for more power, had to be controlled. Subjects, it was ordered, must only take up arms at the King's behest. Duels were forbidden, and many duellists were executed for defying this order. The fortifying of castles was prohibited, to discourage military defiance of central power, with hundreds of fortresses razed to the ground by Richelieu's orders.

Having put down internal disturbances, Richelieu was able to undertake his self-imposed duty of overthrowing the House of Hapsburg. Although he was a cardinal of the Roman Catholic Church, he brought France into the Thirty Years' War on the side of the German Protestant princes, because they were fighting Spain and Austria, the two powers each ruled by a branch of the Hapsburg family and each dangerous to France's security.

Until 1635 the Thirty Years' War had been to a great extent a religious and German struggle, but it had developed into a political contest between rival nations. Richelieu declared war on Spain, making alliances with Sweden and Holland. In 1638 the French occupied Alsace, in the same year winning a great victory over the Spanish in Genoa; and in 1639 a Spanish fleet in the English Channel was destroyed by the Dutch. Richelieu considered that France was secure from invasion for the time being; he had unified the country under the single authority of the King. By the time Mazarin came to power in 1643 Richelieu's policies were beginning to pay off. Austria was no longer a menace to France, and Spain was suffering from internal revolt and facing financial ruin.

Richelieu's administration was marked by the strengthening of the central government in its control over the whole of France. The belief that the King should have absolute authority under God over all his subjects had gradually come to be accepted by the French people. In medieval times a French king had been merely an elected leader among fellow princes of equal status who ruled other provinces in the land - the 'royal domain' around Paris being one of the smallest. Only after long struggles did the French kings emerge by the beginning of the sixteenth century as 'absolute' rulers of the whole of France, passing on their titles to their sons.

Richelieu aimed continuously at the reduction of the power of all the bodies likely to interfere with the authority of the central government. He forbade the *Parlement* of Paris to exercise political functions, and he gradually replaced the governors of provinces with *intendants* who were royal officers appointed by the King, with political, judicial and military duties. They had considerable powers and were also expected to raise money for the Crown and to maintain law and order.

In Louis XIV's reign the peasants represented almost eighty per cent of the total population of around eighteen million. Illiterate and isolated, they existed at almost starvation level, living in thatched hovels and attempting to farm their smallholdings with wooden spades and ploughs of medieval design. La Bruyère, an erudite observer of French society, described them:

> Certain wild creatures, male and female, are to be seen about the countryside; grimy, livid, burnt black by the sun as though tethered to the soil which they dig and till with unconquerable tenacity... When they stand upright, they show a human face; they are in fact men. At night they creep back into dens where they live on black bread, water and roots...

At the other end of the social scale, the *gloire* of France was represented by the *noblesse de l'épée* - the nobility of the sword, the descendants of the old feudal families whose wealth was based on land which they had inherited from their ancestors. They lived on fixed rents paid by peasants on their estates, but by the middle of the seventeenth century their wealth had sunk considerably, due to inflation and the fall in the value of money caused by Spanish gold imports from America. For decades their fortunes had been squandered on maintaining a lifestyle of extravagant splendour, instead of investing in their land and developing agricultural techniques. Because of Richelieu's policies they had been excluded from the royal council. Now, with only their military duties left, they could no longer afford to live on their estates, but were compelled to seek relief by becoming courtiers.

The new power in the land was in the hands of the wealthy, educated middle classes. The French Crown needed able, educated administrators and officials, and money was wanted for the expenses of Court, Government and the continual wars. A member of the bourgeoisie, having made his fortune in business, was only too eager to buy himself a government post. It was even possible to buy 'letters of nobility' from the King, and this too became a way by which the Crown made money. Despised and resented by the hereditary nobles, this new class, the *'noblesse de la robe'*, the nobility of the lawyer's gown, became increasingly powerful as they began to play a large part in the running of the State.

Famine, plague and war, those periodic scourges, were ruining France when Louis XIV came to the throne, and civil war was not far away. The young King was idolised by his subjects. The Queen and the cardinal would often use him to impress the masses, as, mounted on a white horse and dressed in cloth-of-gold, he would ride through the streets of Paris, a spectacle of glory calculated to appeal to the common people. But as soon as he was out of the public eye his impressive robes were replaced by garments he had long grown out of, ragged doublets and stockings full of holes. The expenses of war had reduced the royal family to a state of near poverty.

In comparison, Mazarin was intent on developing his own lifestyle on a grandiose scale to match his increasing fortune. When he built a palatial town-house filled with magnificent art treasures and expensive furniture there was a general outcry against him, and even suggestions that he used black magic to seduce and possess the Queen's mind. Mazarin, however, absorbed in foreign affairs and his own personal life, scorned such evidence that the French people were becoming incensed by the growing power of the monarchy and at being ruled by a Spanish-born Queen and an Italian prime minister. The *intendants* were reducing the power of the local officials throughout the country, while the middle classes resented the heavy taxes they had to pay because of their country's participation in the Thirty Years' War.

All over Europe other countries were suffering from internal conflict. The people of Naples had expelled their viceroy, the Low Countries, freed from Spanish rule, had become a republic, and in England, Charles I had been captured and Parliament was drawing up plans for the Commonwealth. Feelings of discontent were smouldering in France; in 1648 the first of the civil wars broke out. Known as the *Frondes*, they were to make a deep impression on Louis and influence his later behaviour towards the French people.

A *fronde* was literally a catapult or sling used by Paris street urchins to fling missiles into the dry moat that surrounded the city, and to flick stones at the carriages of the rich people. The name *Fronde* was adopted by those who intended to defy authority; calling themselves *Frondeurs*, they wore blue scarves embroidered with a gold sling.

The first *Fronde* was a revolt begun by the *Parlements*. These were bodies of lawyers in Paris and the major provincial cities, who registered and authorised all laws made by the King and council and saw that they were enforced. They also had the right to refuse to register laws to which they were opposed. These wealthy scholars were on the whole completely out of touch with the majority of the populace. They called themselves 'the fathers of the people', but though they were popular with the common people for their flowery speeches advocating liberty and freedom, they were more concerned with protecting their own privileges.

The *Parlement* of Paris now demanded the 'reformation of the Government and the better ordering of the State' and drew up a charter of constitutional rights, including a form of *habeas corpus*, control over taxation and abolition of the *intendants*. Mazarin agreed to some of their demands in order to gain time, but the Queen, who had been brooding over what she considered the *Parlement's* treasonable blackmail, suddenly ordered the arrest of the three main troublemakers, including an elderly magistrate, Pierre Broussel. Broussel was popular with the people of Paris, who rose in sympathy and rioted in the streets shouting 'Broussel! Freedom!'

'The mob has taken up arms' the Queen wrote in a letter. 'The barricades have been put up in the streets.. this is only the beginning; the evil may grow to a point where the royal authority may be destroyed.'

For two days Anne resisted pleas to release Broussel, stating that she would rather strangle him with her own hands than give in to the demands of the mob. As the situation worsened she was persuaded by Mazarin to give in, and reluctantly ordered the old man's release; but the riots continued, and Louis, watching from a window in the Palais Royal, heard the mob denouncing his mother and the 'Italian monkey'. They shouted their allegiance to Louis himself, but fearing they might try and seize the King and hold him as a hostage his mother decided to move the family out of the capital back to the château of Saint-Germain-en-Laye, a few miles from Paris. The move took place secretly at night, and they arrived there to find no beds, linen or furniture. For the next three months the royal home became a near-prison. Madame de Motteville recorded:

> The King's household was in a pitiable state. It was badly supplied; his table was often insufficient. Some of the crown jewels were in pawn; the armies were not equipped; the soldiers, though faithful, were not paid and could not fight. The chief as well as the lesser officers of the household, being left without wages, would no longer serve; the pages of the chamber were sent back to their families because the gentlemen of the chamber had no means of feeding them. The monarchy...was now in a short time reduced to poverty.

Louis never quite forgave his treatment by the people of Paris.

The *Parlement* of Paris refused to register any acts dealing with finances or taxation and would not allow any money to go to the Crown. They demanded further reforms, reduction of taxes, a say in financial policy and no more arrests on the strength of a *lettre de cachet* (a royal order putting a person in prison without trial). 'My son would be little better than a cardboard king if we give in to these demands,' protested Anne. But Mazarin persuaded her to make concessions, and a declaration was signed on 22 September 1648. Two days later the Thirty Years' War was brought to an end by the Treaty of Westphalia. Mazarin's policy had been justified; taxes could be cut and the army could be used if necessary to deal with the rebellious *Parlements*.

Peace was short-lived, however, as almost immediately the second *Fronde* - the *Fronde* of the Princes - began. The members of the nobility, the new *Frondeurs*, were not interested in reform and had no love for the *Parlement* of Paris. Its members had no feelings of patriotism and were little else but trouble-makers and intriguers who wished to get rid of Mazarin and gain control of the country. In 1651 Mazarin had imprisoned three of France's great noblemen, the Duc de Longueville, the Prince de Conti and the Prince de Condé, the 'Grand Master of France' who was the victor of the battle of Rocroi and a national hero. These three, considering that Mazarin was attacking their power and wealth, had raised a private army in Spain and marched on Paris, but had been defeated by Mazarin's troops.

The cause of the three imprisoned princes was taken up by the *Parlement* of Paris. The old and new *Frondeurs* had united against Mazarin, who, realising that his continued presence was doing the King more harm than good, quietly slipped out of the country in the hope that his departure would defuse the situation.

Rumours began to circulate that Gaston d'Orléans, the King's uncle, was planning to seize the King and proclaim himself the Regent. The Queen decided that she must leave Paris again and take the two children to safety, but this time there was no secret departure under the cover of night. Reports of the proposed flight had been circulated through the city and an angry mob gathered outside the Palais Royal. Refusing to accept the fact that the King was still there, they threatened to break down the gates and storm the palace. There was only one thing to be done; the Queen gave orders that the doors should be unlocked. The mob swarmed up the stairs to Louis's bedroom where the boy lay still, fully dressed under the covers, pretending to be asleep. The mob's anger was swiftly replaced by whispered protestations of loyalty to the King and they left 'like gentle subjects, praying God with all their heart to preserve the young prince whose presence, even asleep, had brought them under his spell.'

Mazarin decided it was politic to return to Paris and himself released the three princes, but Condé refused to accept his terms and rode from Le Havre where he had been imprisoned to Paris to take charge of the *Fronde*. Mazarin hastily departed for Germany where he remained for almost a year.

The events of the evening when the mob had invaded his bedroom made a strong and lasting impression on Louis. He disliked the idea of the common people taking any part in the government of the country, believing that absolute rule was the only way of preventing disorder and violence. He had also learned during the second *Fronde* to mistrust the nobility, regarding them as unscrupulous self-seekers and enemies of the monarchy.

On 5 September 1651 he celebrated his thirteenth birthday, and two days later rode to the Palais de Justice. No longer dependent on his mother or the exiled Cardinal Mazarin, he announced to the *Parlement* of Paris, 'Gentlemen, I have come to my *Parlement* to tell you that according to the law of the land I intend to assume the government myself. I hope by the goodness of God I shall govern with piety and justice.' From now on, Louis alone would rule.

It was a great day for France. Crowds massed in the streets as their boy King rode by, dressed in a coat covered in gold embroidery, mounted on a cream-coloured charger, and escorted by a colourful procession of noblemen, officers and Swiss guards. In the houses along the route, ladies leaned from the garlanded windows and threw flowers at the passing cavalcade.

John Evelyn, the English diarist, watching from a friend's house, wrote 'The King went almost the whole way with his hat in his hand, saluting the ladies and acknowledging the acclamations of the crowd who filled the air with shouts of *Vive le Roi!* He seemed a prince of grave yet sweet countenance.. The French are the only nation in Europe to idolise their sovereign.'

During the following *lit de justice*, the procedure which compelled a *Parlement* to register a law, Louis affixed his signature to two edicts, one against duels and blasphemy and the other declaring the great Condé innocent of the charges of making treaties with France's enemies. 'He has the bearing and intelligence of a man of twenty-five' observed one of his courtiers.

Louis's coming-of-age was celebrated with tournaments, ballets and other colourful festivities. His love of the ballet was well known - now he was to dance in public for the first time, appearing in a dazzling costume as the rising sun, on his head a crown of golden rays topped with plumes, miniature suns his knee- and shoe-buckles, and flamelike beams radiating from his body and his hair. Long before he adopted the title of Sun King, Louis was regarded by his subjects as the Sun of France; and as such the possessor of healing powers and possibly also of other magical virtues.

The *Fronde* of the Princes continued for another two years. Condé had ignored the King's edict declaring him innocent, and had deliberately stayed away from the coming-of-age festivities. Declaring war on France at large, he departed for Bordeaux, determined to detach his estates from France and declare himself ruler of a separate kingdom.

At Louis's request, Mazarin returned from exile with four thousand mercenaries in his own pay. The King and his godfather were reunited after eleven months, and greeted each other affectionately. Louis was now to receive his first taste of battle -

albeit at a safe distance from the fighting.

Condé had announced his intention of taking Paris. Louis, with Mazarin at his side, watched from the hills of Charonne. Condé's army entered Paris, but his triumph was short-lived. Two days later, the princes, quarrelling as usual with the authorities, incited the mob to set fire to the Town Hall, killing several members of the *Parlement*. The *Parlement* of Paris, the mob and the majority of the nobles were weary of war and turned against the princes. The Parisians hated the Spanish troops Condé had brought to occupy the capital. In October, Condé was forced to flee from Paris. Mazarin again made a temporary diplomatic departure for Germany and the Vicomte de Turenne, who had become a *Frondeur* for love of Condé's sister, now came back to the side of the King and became one of Louis's greatest military advisors.

On 21 October 1652 the King and his court triumphantly entered Paris, welcomed with shouts of loyalty by the fickle crowd. The next day a general amnesty was proclaimed, and the *Fronde* was finished after four years of chaos and bitterness.

The Sun Rises

1654 – 1661

ON 7 JUNE 1654 the sun shone brilliantly for the Sun King's coronation in Rheims Cathedral.

He entered the great Cathedral on foot, preceded by a stately procession headed by the Grand Provost of France; musicians playing all manner of instruments, velvet-clad, their tabards powdered with fleur-de-lis, the lily-emblems of France; halberd-bearers, and officials escorting the golden mace. Before the congregation and the Bishop of Soissons, Louis promised to defend and observe the rights of the Catholic Church, and pronounced the Coronation Oath: to promise that all Christian people should maintain the true Peace of God's Church, by the will of his Government, that he would forbid all violence and unjust acts among his subjects, and that justice and mercy should be used in all judgments. He was fifteen years old.

At the end of the long, elaborate ceremony of prayer, blessing and anointing, he sat at last in view of all, on the ancient throne of King Dagobert, high-placed above the body of the Cathedral, beneath the great rose-window. The crown of Charlemagne was on his head, the sceptre and the gold-and-ivory Hand of Justice in his hands. His ermine-trimmed ceremonial robe spread about him, on his feet were shoes of velvet, and golden spurs set with garnets, signifying that the King was also a soldier, just as his violet tunic and mantle signified that he was in part a priest.

As the Cathedral doors were flung open, fowlers in the galleries released five hundred white doves to swirl and flutter above the glittering figure on Dagobert's throne. Outside the crowds cheered and shouted, bells rang joyfully from the towers, the royal sword called Joyeuse pointed upwards towards God. But Louis, today, was second to God in the eyes of his people. The most resplendent monarch in all history had begun his reign as he meant to continue it, in glory spiritual and temporal.

Two days later Louis appeared at his first public ceremony as crowned King. In the park of the Abbey of Saint-Remi two thousand men, women and children awaited his arrival. These unfortunates were all suffering from a form of tuberculosis of the glands of the neck known as scrofula or 'King's Evil'. Their belief was that only the King himself had the power to cure this disease, and as the sufferers slowly filed past him Louis touched each one, making the sign of the cross on their face and repeating 'The King touches thee, God heals thee.' That they were cured is unlikely, but comforted they certainly were.

Louis's training in politics and statecraft was intensified. Each day he would visit Mazarin in the cardinal's magnificent apartments, where they would go through the latest dispatches together, Louis asking questions and Mazarin testing him and discussing why one course of action was preferable to another. He taught Louis all he knew of European affairs, and from him the boy also learned the art of leadership, the use of subtle diplomacy and the ability to play on the rivalries and weaknesses of others.

His general education was of a fairly low standard. He had little enthusiasm for books, preferring to spend all his free time in physical activities. Each morning he would exercise in his gymnasium, fencing, drilling with pike or musket, and vaulting with 'wonderful agility'. Dancing was one of his great pleasures and skills; he had ballet lessons regularly with a professional ballet-master.

Louis was devoted to his mother, and she to him. He spent several hours a day in her company, joining her for breakfast and staying with her while she dressed, after which ritual they would attend Mass together. Anne had been responsible for her son's religious guidance since childhood and had passed on her devout Catholic faith to Louis. She was extremely ignorant of theology, having only two beliefs - that no one could disagree with a king appointed by God, and that it was the royal duty to crush heretics.

Louis never showed any interest in religious study, believing that kings did not settle theological problems; they only enforced the decisions which the Church dictated. His was not a spiritual nature, and spirituality was in any case unfashionable.

Afternoons were spent in hunting, shooting or playing *jeu de paume* (tennis), after which Louis would drive along the avenue of horse-chestnut trees which lined the royal promenade by the Seine, where he could see and be seen by his subjects. 'One cannot sufficiently admire the incessant activity of our young monarch' commented *La Gazette*. His energies were indeed boundless. Plays, ballets, and other entertainments were presented in the evenings to amuse him, and he also enjoyed sessions with his friends, telling stories and performing mimes. He was a passionate gambler, following the examples of his mother and godfather; the three of them spent hours playing cards or *hoca*, an early form of roulette.

The young King's other passion was war. From his mid-teens he had formed the habit of visiting his armies every spring. In the company of the great general Turenne he watched the fighting during the battles against the Spanish at Dunkirk and Mardyke in 1658. He was eager to make his mark as a soldier, but Mazarin held him back, arguing that the person of the King was more valuable to France than all her armies combined. He picked up a fever, probably typhoid, which was as nearly fatal as a bullet. Luckily his strong constitution survived the ministrations of the doctors, who frequently killed more patients than they cured.

As the King matured his mother took a hand in a new aspect of his education. Contemporary gossip said that Anne had selected one of her own ladies of the bedchamber, a forty-year-old widow, Madame de Beauvais, to initiate her son 'into the rites of

Venus'. She was said to have waylaid the sixteen-year-old King on his way from the bath, or in the attics of the Louvre. 'The Old Circe' as Saint-Simon calls her in his *Mémoires*, must have pleased the boy, as she and her family enjoyed particular prestige at Court for the rest of her life - though the experience was never repeated.

Louis was now ready for further sexual encounters and these came readily, for few females could resist the charisma of the handsome King. His sister-in-law, the second Duchesse d'Orléans, was to write of him later in one of her innumerable letters, 'The King was gallant, often to the point of debauch. Anyone at all would do just so long as she was female…just so that she gave the impression of loving him… It made no difference to him whether she was a lady of quality, a chamberwoman or a gardener's daughter.'

Unfortunately, according to the royal medical journal, the King soon suffered the consequences of his excesses; he contacted gonorrhea. His physician warned him of the consequences venereal diseases might have on his heirs, which knowledge, coupled with Louis's disgust and embarrassment at having the disease, and the unpleasant treatment it involved, made him concentrate for some time on purely chaste romantic affairs with no physical involvement.

It was inevitable that he should eventually fall genuinely in love. His choice fell on one of the young nieces Mazarin had sent for from Italy so that they might make good marriages in France. They were Laure, Olympe, Hortense, Marie, Anne and Marie-Anne (to use the French version of their Italian names). Three of the 'Mazarinettes' look out from a painting by an unknown and fairly primitive artist, strongly Italian in features, bold-eyed, full-lipped and inclined to double chins, but Marie, whose Diana costume hints at the sporting interests she shared with Louis, is the prettiest of the three. He may have fancied Olympe at first, but Marie captured his heart seriously; in any case, Mazarin had hurriedly married Olympe off to the Comte de Soissons. Marie was lively, well-read, and may have been either a little in love with Louis or determined to share his throne. She wept at his bedside when he was seriously ill with fever, she cheered his convalescence. There were idyllic picnics at Fontainebleau, water-parties on the lake. Louis was happy in Marie's company, livelier than anyone had yet seen him. Descriptions of him at this time reflect his own great attractions: bright blue-grey eyes, fine mouth, cleft chin (supposed to denote an amorous disposition), brown waving hair, and physical grace. Marie Mancini must have had glowing hopes.

The obvious policy for Mazarin would have been to bring off a brilliant alliance between his niece and the King. But that was not his aim. Louis must marry for France, and preferably marry Spain; he and Marie must part. He might write to her, but that was all (and the letters were opened and read). There was a last unhappy meeting at St-Jean d'Angély, he gave her a puppy to remember him by; a few more letters were exchanged, and that was the end. Marie became Princess of Colonna. Her reputation as the girl beloved by a king had caused Colonna some misgivings, and he was apparently surprised to find that his bride was a virgin.

The Queen had long wished for a reconciliation between France and Spain, the country of her birth. Her great ambition was for Louis to marry the elder daughter of the Spanish King Philip IV. That Maria Teresa was already promised to the Emperor of Germany was a complication, but Mazarin laid his plans carefully, determined to get the Infanta for France. For five months he and the Spanish prime minister worked on the terms for the marriage and peace between their two countries, culminating in the signing of the Peace of the Pyrenees on 7 November 1659, which marked the replacement of Spain by France as the foremost power in Europe. The treaty included a marriage contract between Louis and Maria Teresa, whose dowry of five hundred thousand crowns was to be paid within eighteen months. If it were not paid, the Infanta should retain her claim to the Spanish throne. The wily Mazarin knew that Spain was virtually bankrupt, with little chance of paying the debt; consequently Louis, through his wife, would have claim to the Spanish Netherlands and even the Spanish throne itself.

The royal wedding was fixed for June 1660. On the sixth of June, Louis and his mother travelled to the Island of Pheasants on the Bidassoa river, and here on neutral territory the Court of France and the Court of Spain assembled. After forty-six years, Queen Anne was to meet her brother Philip of Spain. The Spaniards, all dressed in black, appeared formal and haughty in comparison with the colourful French, with their frivolous conduct, gay beribboned clothes and flowing ringlets. Anne approached her brother to greet him with a kiss, but Spanish etiquette and the King's awesome pomposity forbade such intimacy. Recoiling from her salute he acknowledged her with a formal touch on the arms.

Louis and his courtiers were amused at their solemn counterparts, but he was intrigued to observe his prospective bride, who was sitting in another hall. He was somewhat taken aback at the sight of the tiny blonde creature, so unlike the voluptuous French ladies in their gaudy finery; so unlike the raven-haired, dark-eyed Marie who was still the only woman he felt he could ever love. Velasquez captured Maria Teresa's likeness unflatteringly at this time. Her dress seems to belong more to the sixteenth century than to her own day, with its square farthingale, boned stomacher and the ugly cape-neck concealing her shoulders (French ladies bared theirs to the limit, occasionally beyond it). Her hair is padded squarely out, leaving the brow bare, its tortured curls ending in what appears to be a fringe of corks: they are, in fact, tassels. Her face is fair, babyish, even slightly porcine. She looks rather stupid. Louis told the Prince de Conti that he thought he could love his bride, but it is unlikely that he meant it, or that he ever did, in any sense, love her. Spanish princesses introduced into foreign courts seldom proved to be great successes. Like Katherine of Aragon before her, and Catherine of Braganza after her, she was accustomed to more stiff and formal manners than were practised by her adopted country. She was too pious and serious, and, for Louis, much too un-French. Her bad pronunciation would always irritate him, her company bore him.

Madame de Motteville summed up the new Queen in her condescending manner: 'With more height and handsomer teeth she would deserve to be estimated one of the most beautiful persons in Europe. Her bosom appeared to be well formed and tolerably full, but her dress was horrible!' Compared with the vivacious, voluptuous and voluble women around her, Marie Thérèse, as she was now known, was very, very dull.

After the initial ceremony in Spain, the couple met officially for the first time at the altar of the little church of St Jean de Luz, where the marriage was solemnized.

The eyes of France were upon the Queen, and comments, particularly those of the ladies, were none too complimentary. However, the marriage made a promising start. Louis was in good spirits and Marie Thérèse was unusually gay, probably more so than she would ever be again. They travelled across France, fêted in every town by their loyal subjects, and after a month resting in the castle of Vincennes they returned to Paris at the end of August for a triumphal procession, the most lavish public show of the century.

Dressed in cloth of gold stitched with pearls and wearing all the crown jewels, the young Queen rode in an open carriage of gold that shone as brightly as the sun itself. Riding beside her through streets strewn with fresh flowers and sweet-smelling herbs was Louis, mounted on a prancing bay stallion, magnificent in silver lace sewn with rubies and pearls and trimmed with pink ribbons. Outside the Hôtel de Beauvais he reined in his horse, and swept off his red and white plumed hat in a flourishing salute to his mother and Cardinal Mazarin, who were seated on the garlanded balcony. 'The Cardinal's suite was the most magnificent in the cavalcade', reported the Venetian ambassador. 'Even the mules' harness was of solid silver and plated gold.' His household took more than an hour to pass in procession, but Mazarin himself was not able to take an active part;

suffering from cancer and gout, he was a very sick man in his hour of glory.

Madame Scarron, a lady who was later to play a major part in Louis's life, wrote to a friend in the provinces, 'The Queen must have gone to bed last night well pleased with the husband she has chosen.' This was something of an understatement: Marie Thérèse had conceived a violent passion for the King, 'an inordinate, an indecorous amorousness' which Louis found highly embarrassing. Though he played the devoted husband for a few weeks he soon began to find her company tedious. Her stilted, accented conversation lacked the sparkle and wit that was expected in Court circles. She was devoted to her aunt the Queen Mother, and would run to her for comfort if anything upset her. The two were drawn together by their mutual language and their devoutness. More and more they gave up their spare time to good works and visiting convents. Louis, though always polite and considerate to Marie Thérèse, spent less and less time in her company.

Mazarin was fatally ill. He had completed Richelieu's work by giving France - 'that square and enclosed field', as Richelieu had described it - a leading place in Europe, and saved the Bourbon throne from hostile rivals. During his last days the cardinal gave the King his final instructions, 'Sire.. never have a Prime Minister. Govern! Let the politicians be a servant, never a master... If you take the government into your own hands, you will do more in one day than a minister cleverer than I in six months.'

Louis never forgot the advice, and lost no time in acting on it. Mazarin died on 9 March 1661. He was fifty-nine. At his bedside was the woman who had ruled the country with him only a few years earlier and whose relationship with him was always to remain a matter for conjecture. Louis wept at the death of his friend and godfather, the man who had guided him through childhood and trained him for his place as King. Now at last the moment of true sovereignty had come. 'I realised' Louis wrote in his Memoirs 'that I was King; for that I had been born. I was transfused with sweet exaltation.' The day after Mazarin's funeral he astonished his incredulous Court by announcing that he would in future take personal control of all State affairs. When officials asked him to whom they should apply about national business he replied simply 'To me'. He told his Secretaries of State, 'I order you not to sign anything, not even a passport, without my command. You shall inform me of everything day by day and favour no one.'

This command was not taken very seriously; even his own mother was said to have laughed out loud. The image of the *'roi fainéant'*, the lazy king, suited only to feasts, ceremonies and frivolities, was taken for granted. After all, Louis XIII had left the government of the State to his Prime Minister. But Louis XIV had lived through civil wars and the disruption that followed. His present and future credibility rested on his ability to govern the most powerful nation in Europe, and the most densely populated: there were eighteen million Frenchmen to England's population of five and a half million.

The King discontinued the big council. Three experienced administrators formed the nucleus of his governmental advisers: Michel Le Tellier for military affairs, Hugues de Lionne, the foreign policy expert, and Nicolas Fouquet, in charge of finance and also as Attorney General. Fouquet's position was far from secure. The King, warned against him by Mazarin, had started an investigation of Fouquet's accounts, which was to have disastrous consequences for the minister in due course.

Louis now devoted himself to what he called 'the calling of a king' and thus became the first French sovereign to make the monarchy a serious profession. He was not an outstandingly clever man, but he was industrious, setting aside from six to eight hours for State affairs, allowing nothing to interrupt his working day. His energy was boundless, his enjoyment of power total.

While the King absorbed himself in his work, the Queen was dedicating herself to charitable affairs. Never the most stimulating of companions, and now suffering the early stages of an uncomfortable pregnancy, Marie Thérèse was a poor mate for her ebullient husband, who found it increasingly difficult to conceal his boredom in her presence. It was inevitable that he would start to seek the company of other women.

With the Court at Fontainebleau in the summer of 1661 was the King's brother Philippe - 'Monsieur' - and his new wife Henriette Anne, sister of Charles II of England. Once dismissed by Louis as a 'bag of bones from the Holy Innocents' cemetery', 'Madame' had developed from a skinny young girl into a tall, graceful woman with a 'roses and jasmine' complexion, blue eyes and chestnut hair. Born with all the graces and an infinite power to please, her sunny temperament and brilliant wit was irresistible to the King who spent most of his time in her company. She was a Stuart, with the irresistible Stuart magic in her, and an extra infusion of elegance from her French mother. To her brother Charles II she was 'Minette', the Kitten, the sister he loved more dearly than any of his mistresses. It was impossible not to love her - except for her husband. If Louis's marriage was dull, Madame's was a disaster. Monsieur's homosexual tendencies were well known, and he had little interest in his beautiful wife. His marital duties quickly bacame tedious; he reverted to the company of his 'mignons', the spiteful Chevalier de Lorraine, 'beautiful as an angel', and the vicious, insolent Comte de Guiche, leaving his bride to find her own diversions.

Louis, who still loved his frivolous effeminate brother, appreciated Madame's plight and set out to entertain her, planning parties and diversions, accompanying her when she went bathing in the Seine (both decorously enveloped in linen shifts), and spending romantic evenings with her in the company of the other beautiful people of the Court. Inevitably, the rumours began to circulate. Madame de La Fayette observed:

> Since they were both infinitely attractive individuals and both born with a disposition to gallantry, and since they were thrown together daily in the

midst of pleasuring and entertainment, it appeared to everyone that they were in that state of intense emotional involvement which is the fore-
runner of a grand passion... There was no doubt
in anyone's mind that there was far more between
them than mere friendship.

The Queen sulked, the Queen Mother remonstra-
ted, but Louis's reaction was to withdraw from
their company, leaving them both frustrated and
furious. The Queen Mother was not a lady to let
such a situation get out of hand. If the King must
stray from the path of marital faithfulness it had
better not be with one who was his first cousin as
well as his sister-in-law. There were other beauties
at Court to be thrown in his way, and his mother
saw to it that they were.

Of the chosen decoys, it was Mademoiselle
Louise de la Vallière who caught the King's eye,
and his heart. His mother's fairly innocent plan
had proved all too successful.

Not Unequal to Many

1661 – 1666

LOUISE DE LA VALLIÈRE was seventeen, a soldier's daughter, country-born. She was fair-haired, blue-eyed, fresh-faced, fond of sports. In the portrait the Comte de Brienne painted of her as Diana she looks like an English schoolgirl. At a Court where dark French beauty was the norm Louise must have seemed like a white violet in a peony-bed.

In that summer of 1661 Louise and Louis went riding, and walking, in the gardens of romantic Fontainebleau, and in the grounds of his father's old hunting-lodge at Versailles, a modest little house in country abounding in game.

As the affaire progressed La Vallière had to suffer the indignities of a hole-and-corner love-life in isolated rooms and borrowed beds in the Tuileries or the Palais Royal, but this state of things was compensated for by the idyllic love she shared with the King, and the enforced secrecy which added excitement to their meetings. She was several times a victim of malicious plots to discredit her. Many of the ladies were in love with the King, envious of the young girl who spent so much time in his company. Besides his overpowering good looks, he had an air of authority and a commanding presence. There was a dignity and grace in his bearing, and though his usual expression was somewhat serious, he had a sense of humour. Bernini's marble bust of him, made in 1665, shows far better than the portraits the utterly self-confident poise of his head, the expression

49

of one who takes his own charm and authority for granted; and, as some have said, an almost theatrical air.

'Every single lady at Court has the ambition to become the King's mistress' wrote Primi Visconti. Louise had to face her would-be rivals every day, including Madame, who had discovered what was going on and who referred nastily to Louise as 'the King's strumpet'. Marie Thérèse was jealous; the Queen Mother made an hysterical scene and threatened to retire into a convent. Louis invited her to do just that, at which she quickly changed her mind. La Vallière suffered greatly, but in her desire not to cause trouble for her lover was prepared to put up with insults and unpleasantness. She was a natural masochist; Louis, perhaps unconsciously, took advantage of this. A considerate man in most relationships, he did not appear to realise that life for his unofficial mistress was none too happy when he was not at her side. He also had other affairs, not of the heart, to occupy much of his attention.

He was engaged in a crucial political battle. He had appointed Jean Baptiste Colbert as assistant to Fouquet, the Superintendent of Finances and Attorney General, with instructions to watch him and collect evidence of suspected fraudulent activities. Within a few weeks Colbert proved conclusively that every afternoon Fouquet was giving the King falsified accounts.

Nicolas Fouquet, handsome womaniser and brilliant politician, had been in office since 1653. At times of crisis he was always able to raise huge sums of money for the Treasury, but although Mazarin had relied on him as one of his most valuable ministers he did not trust him. Fouquet was an avid collector of priceless objets d'art, coins, statues and rare manuscripts, and his three country houses were set in landscaped gardens and filled with expensive furniture, pictures, tapestries and other treasures, beyond the scope of his apparent fortune. A dangerous man to cross, Fouquet had friends and spies everywhere; as his wealth grew so did his power, and his supporters were convinced that when the King's interest in politics began to pall he would appoint Fouquet Prime Minister and leave the business of government to him. The ambitious superintendent intended to live up to his family motto 'To what heights will he not climb?' He was sure that one day France would be in his hands. He would follow in the footsteps of Richelieu and Mazarin - Louis XIV would be just another royal figurehead.

Fouquet underestimated the King. Louis had been instructed well by the crafty cardinal; he was determined to bring Fouquet down with Colbert's help. He trapped the unsuspecting superintendent into relinquishing his post of attorney general, hinting that he would then be able to become controller, another step towards the post of Prime Minister. In fact, in the event of his arrest, Fouquet would then be unable to stand trial before his influential friends in the *Parlement*, but would be tried by a special court. Fouquet fell into the trap and sold the office of attorney general for the equivalent of almost half a million pounds, which he presented to the King, hoping to ensure his continuing favour. Complimenting himself on his diplomacy and dreaming of his dazzling future, he invited King and Court to a celebration at his château, Vaux-le-Vicomte, about thirty miles from Paris.

The château, designed by the leading architect Louis le Vau, was magnificent, the furnishings and decorations priceless and Le Nôtre's gardens breathtaking in their beauty and design. Nothing like it had ever been seen before in France, eclipsing even the royal palaces. Louis, smiling and courteous as ever to his host, was inwardly raging, knowing that all this splendour had been bought with money stolen from the State and from him personally.

Two weeks later a Captain d'Artagnan and his company of Musketeers approached Fouquet after a council meeting, to inform him that the King had ordered his arrest. Everyone was taken by surprise and Fouquet was thunderstruck. He had received warnings from friends, but ignored them, believing himself to be above suspicion. His trial lasted for three years, until, found guilty, he was sentenced to life imprisonment in the fortress of Pignerol on the Italian border. Vaux-le-Vicomte was sold to pay the enormous fines, and Louis appropriated many of its treasures for himself, on the grounds that they had been paid for out of public money.

For all their severity, Fouquet's fines did not go far towards alleviating the nation's finances. The national debt in 1661 was £143 million, and the King's income £72 million a year. When Colbert had helped to overthrow Fouquet he took his place as superintendent, later to be controller general. Jean-Baptiste Colbert was an intimidating character known as 'The North' or 'the man of marble' because of his icy temperament and severe colourless personality. He set no great store by friendship, did not like public attention, and loathed the Church, regarding priests and monks as idle themselves and encouraging idleness in others by their indiscriminate charity. He was, however, a brilliant administrator and wholeheartedly devoted to the service of the King. Working conscientiously from five in the morning, he would stay at his desk for anything up to sixteen hours in his determination to make France prosperous and independent.

Colbert's plan was to modernise the French economy and encourage the people to become more industrious like the Dutch, the richest community in Europe. France desperately needed to develop her industries and become self-supporting. The cloth trade was reorganised so that it could compete successfully in the markets of the Levant, millions of acres of forest were protected from indiscriminate felling to conserve supplies of timber, and in 1667 the tariff on all important foreign imports was doubled.

Colbert's first step was to reform the tax system. The poorest in the land had to pay several taxes. There was the *taille* based on a man's income from the land he owned, there were taxes on certain products, the *aides* were levied on wines and spirits and the *gabelle* on salt, which everyone was forced to buy in large quantities. Only the nobility and the clergy were exempt from these taxes. Colbert, having discovered that tax-collectors stole two-thirds of the money they collected, forced them to keep stricter accounts, with the result that by 1667 the King's income from taxes had doubled.

While trying to reduce the burden on the poor, Colbert also tackled the King's own expenses, an unpopular project, as it insisted on a reduction in spending on parties and other entertainments and a cut-back of new building plans.

In December 1663 Louise had given birth to a son by the King, and six months later the most magnificent fête so far was held at Versailles in celebration, though officially it was in honour of the birth of a Dauphin to Marie-Thérèse in November. Entitled *The Pleasures of the Enchanted Isle*, it consisted of pageants, plays and sports. Noblemen dressed as knights in armour competed in an arena in the *course de bague*, catching rings off a pole with their lances as they galloped past. At nightfall the arena was lit by four thousand torches and supper was announced by the Four Seasons, Spring on a great Spanish horse, Summer on an elephant, Autumn on a camel and Winter on a bear. The Seasons were accompanied by twelve gardeners, twelve reapers, twelve wine harvesters and twelve old men. They indicated the difference between the Seasons by flowers, wheatsheafs, fruits and mirrors, and carried on their heads great bowls in which were heaped the ingredients of the collation which was to follow. The god Pan appeared in the person of the rising playwright Molière.

During the fête Louis himself performed in a ballet, mounted, as the official account states, 'on one of the finest horses in the world, whose flame-coloured harness glittered with gold and silver and precious stones. His Majesty was armoured in the fashion of the Greeks, like everyone else in his quadrille, wearing a cuirass of silver plate covered with rich embroidery of gold and diamonds. His bearing and his whole behaviour were worthy of his rank; his helmet, all covered with flame-coloured plumes, had an incomparable grace.'

The spectacular fêtes which were such a feature of Louis XIV's reign were a particular drain on the country's finances. One of the most famous was a great tilting match on the huge space in front of the Tuileries which was afterwards known as the Place Carousel. As a result of the Carousel, an 'extraordinary entertainment', a medal was designed depicting the sun rising over the globe and bearing the inscription *Nec Pluribus Impar*, Not Unequal to Many. For ever afterwards Louis XIV was known as the Sun King, his glory as great abroad as in his own country.

The splendour of Versailles would provide Louis with a setting for his temple dedicated to the cult of monarchy. 'A palace befitting my grandeur' as he had said. Work was already started on converting the 'Little House of Cards' into a great palace, a constant reminder of some of the happiest days in the King's life.

Anne the Queen Mother died in January 1666. She had been suffering from cancer of the breast, and for six months every remedy had been tried. Louis mourned her deeply, but her strict religious principles had been getting more and more oppressive, casting a gloom over the *joie de vivre* of Court life. At last he was able to give Louise de la Vallière the recognition and status she had lacked for so long. Louise was now the King's official mistress, and their little daughter Marie Anne was legitimised.

That October, La Vallière gave birth to another daughter. While she was recovering from her confinement the King visited her often at the Hôtel Brion, the little house he had given her in the grounds of the Palais Royal. Though he still loved her dearly, he was beginning to find his mistress's simple sweetness a trifle cloying. At the age of twenty-six and after three pregnancies Louise's girlish prettiness was beginning to fade. Aware of her limitations as a bright and witty conversationalist, she surrounded herself with ladies who could help her entertain her royal lover.

Amongst these was one of whom it had once been said by her own cousin, 'She had designs on the King's heart and started laying her plans from the day she came to Court.' Her name was Athénaïs de Montespan.

Love and War

1666 – 1674

ATHÉNAÏS DE MONTESPAN was twenty-six, haughty and arrogant. 'A consummate beauty,' commented Mme de La Fayette, 'and yet, somehow, for some reason, not entirely appealing.' She was proud and extravagant, the wife of a wild roisterer, the Gascon Marquis de Montespan, who spent more time on endless military campaigns than with his wife. A daughter had been born in 1664 and a son the following year, but the marriage was already foundering on the rocks of bankruptcy, incompatibility and lengthy separations.

Born Françoise de Rochechouart in 1640, Athénaïs was of stock as ancient and illustrious as any in France. Her father, the Duc de Mortemart, was First Gentleman of the King's bedchamber, her mother lady-in-waiting to Anne, the Queen Mother, and her brother Louis had been gentleman-in-waiting to the King since they were both seven years old. Françoise and her three sisters were sent to a convent school until they were old enough to join the rest of the family at Court. At that time there was a vogue for classical names. Deciding that Françoise was too common, she adopted the name Athénaïs. Her debut at Court at the age of twenty-one created a ripple of admiration. 'One of the most beautiful people in the world,' observed the Comte de Bussy, her cousin. 'Her beauty a magnet to the eyes and a stimulus to the lusts of all the gallants of the Court.' The something 'not entirely appealing' about her is apparent in a portrait showing her as Iris (now at Versailles). The heavy-lidded eyes glint with humour, but there is something smug and self-satisfied about the set of the full-lipped pursed mouth, and a predatory look to the plump hands touching the gauzy scarf spun by the rainbow.

Certainly Athénaïs, like most of the other Court ladies, had experienced romantic longings for the King, but his eyes were only for La Vallière, and in 1663 Athénaïs allowed herself to be swept off her feet by the handsome swashbuckling de Montespan. Two years later, disillusioned with marriage and bored with motherhood, she became close friends with the Comtesse de Soissons, formerly Olympe Mancini, and Madame, both former mistresses of the King and both persistent intriguers playing dangerous games, manipulating people and spreading scandalous tales about everyone at Court. Being what they were, the three fell out with each other. When Madame quarrelled with her effeminate husband, Athénaïs took his side and was forthwith barred from Madame's presence. Happily for her she was then made lady-in-waiting to the Queen, so her chance had at last come to gain the King's attention.

Louis was not attracted by her at first. He is said to have commented to Monsieur, 'She tried hard but I'm not interested.' But Athénaïs, who was shrewd and cunning, made herself invaluable to the Queen, taking Communion in her company every week, giving an impression of virtuousness which the pious Marie Thérèse found appealing. When La Vallière was recovering from her confinement and innocently invited her old friend to keep her company and help to entertain the King, Athénaïs accepted eagerly.

By November the Duc d'Enghien was writing to the Queen of Poland, telling of a significant development in the King's love life. 'He has apparently taken a fancy to her (Mme de Montespan) and to tell the truth she would well merit an interest, for it is impossible to have more wit and beauty than she. Not that there is as yet anything definite to point to...'

Throughout the winter it was obvious that Louis's interest in Athénaïs was growing. In the following

May when he left Saint-Germain to spend the summer with his troops, he was accompanied by a number of courtiers, the Queen and the Queen's ladies, among them Mme de Montespan. War had flared up between France and Spain once again. Mazarin's suspicion that the Queen's dowry would never be paid appeared to be confirmed. The marriage contract had stipulated that in such an event Marie Thérèse would retain her rights to certain Spanish possessions in the Netherlands. Philip of Spain had died in 1665. Basing his claim on the details of the marriage contract, Louis began what came to be known as the Queen's War - the war of the Spanish Devolution.

In May 1667 French troops under the command of Turenne entered Belgian Flanders. They found little resistance and spent some time besieging strongholds which fell into their hands easily. The King and his Court departed to join the army in the Netherlands. Voltaire describes the royal progress: 'The ruin of the Dutch was planned during this voyage in the midst of entertainments. It was a continuous fête in a setting of utmost splendour.'

The King, who until then had made all his military expeditions on horseback, this time travelled for the first time in a coach with glass windows. The Queen, Madame, and the Marquise de Montespan were in this superb vehicle, followed by many others, and when Mme de Montespan travelled alone four lifeguardsmen were stationed at the doors of her coach. The Dauphin and his court followed, and Mademoiselle, the King's cousin, with hers. The most beautiful furniture was taken from the Court to the towns where the parties spent the night; in each one there was a masked ball or fireworks. In effect the Court of France went on tour like a theatrical company through the provinces into neighbouring and conquered territories. The war was one long triumphal procession. In two and a half months the French had captured the chain of Spanish fortresses, most of whose defenders had been recalled to Spain, and Louis invited the Queen and her ladies to join him on the battlefield to enjoy the spectacle of their King leaping sword in hand across the open trenches.

It was during the summer of 1668 that Athénaïs and the King became lovers. The story goes that one night he had bribed her ladies to retire to their quarters and, disguised in the uniform of a Swiss Guard, had appeared in Athénaïs's bedroom. Louise de la Vallière had been left behind in France. Five months pregnant, distressed about the developing relationship between her lover and her friend, she had not been comforted by the title of duchess which the King bestowed on her before he left on his campaign: she remarked that it put her in mind of a present given to a faithful servant on retirement. The reason why she later decided to join the royal party in Holland is not known. Perhaps it was just the whim of a pregnant, unhappy woman who wanted desperately to be with the father of her children and to reassure herself, or at least to know the worst about the King's conduct.

There was a distressing scene on the arrival of the discarded favourite. The exhausted woman and her two attendants sat weeping on their trunks. The Queen was distraught, and Mme de Montespan was loud in professed indignation: 'Heaven preserve me from ever becoming the King's mistress, but were such a fate to befall me I would never be so brazen as to face the Queen.' Next day, La Vallière, snubbed by the Queen and pitied by the rest of the company, made the only defiant gesture of her life and galloped her carriage ahead of the Queen to greet Louis on his return from the battlefield. Later she wrote in her *Reflections on the Mercy of God* that she had been 'dragged along as if by wild horses' by her desperate love for the King. Marie Thérèse was hysterical with rage, but Louis calmed her down, and La Vallière was allowed to join the Queen and her ladies for dinner that night and to ride with the Queen to Mass on the following day. The three women were continually thrown together because of the demands of protocol. Although the King's attitude towards his former favourite was kind, he encouraged the Queen's jealousy of her so that suspicion would not fall upon Athénaïs. 'The Queen's confusion as to the identity of her husband's latest light-of-love was a

Court joke,' commented Mademoiselle. 'People laughed about it with the King.'

Gradually Athénaïs began to excuse herself from the Queen's company on various pretexts, no longer accompanying her on promenades or to Mass. Marie Thérèse may not have realised, but everyone else certainly did, that her husband's affaire with her lady-in-waiting was becoming more and more serious; in fact the two of them were regularly sleeping together. La Vallière was forced to continue her rôle as mistress-in-chief in order to try to hide the King's new love affaire from the rest of the world.

Louis's behaviour was unforgiveable, but the gentle Louise's meek acceptance of her lot seemed to bring out a sadistic streak in his nature. La Vallière carried her masochistic participation in the plot to the lengths of continuing her friendship with de Montespan. The extraordinary ménage-à-quatre delighted the scandalmongers of the Court. Athénaïs dyed her hair blonde because the Queen and Louise were natural blondes; Marie Thérèse adopted the de Montespan hair style because she knew the King admired it; Louise dressed and curled her rival's hair, entwining it with pearls and ribbons; the three women went everywhere together, often accompanied by the King. Mme de Sévigné wrote 'The Dew and the Torrent (La Vallière and de Montespan) are linked by mutual confidence and every day they see the Fire and the Snow (the King and the Queen). This cannot last long without causing great disorder.' But the situation continued for six years.

What of the absent husband, the aggressive, violent and explosive Marquis de Montespan? He came storming into Paris, burst into his wife's apartment at Saint-Germain, boxed her ears and disappeared again. Rumours circulated to the effect that he and a friend were planning to abduct Athénaïs and carry her off to Spain. After several more violent scenes the King ordered the Marquis's arrest and after a few weeks' imprisonment he was banished to his estates. In 1669 he returned from exile to stage a macabre mock funeral for his wife, informing his friends that Athénaïs had died from 'coquetry and ambition'. The Montespan children, aged five and three, accompanied their father to the elaborate ghoulish ceremony dressed in formal mourning clothes. Then the Marquis disappeared into exile again, taking the children with him, apparently with no word of protest from Athénaïs, who seemed glad to be rid of them. She had by that time given birth to the first of her babies by the King. Two years later the Marquis was pardoned and returned to France, giving the Court a wide berth and settling down to a more or less blameless life. Louis even offered him a dukedom, but he refused in order to deny Athénaïs her ambition to become a duchess.

Louis dreamed of restoring the huge empire of his ancestor Charlemagne, the first Holy Roman Emperor, who 'made the French name the terror of the whole earth'. Louis XIV was to write that Charlemagne's empire had been won 'by courage and by victories which are the choice and the votes of Heaven itself when it has resolved to subordinate the other powers to a single one.' He himself saw Europe as 'a vast arena that offered great opportunities for me to distinguish myself and fulfil the great expectations that I had for some time inspired in the public.'

Louis's two Ministers of War, Michel le Tellier and his son the Marquis de Louvois, were responsible for the reforms that transformed the French army from a ravaging gang of mercenary soldiers and amateur bandits, seeking a prime opportunity for raiding and looting, into a disciplined band of professionals. The King himself became Commander-in-Chief in 1661, and from then on the army became 'a career open to the talented'. Promotion had to be won by merit instead of being bought, provision was made for the troops' welfare; regular pay, tough discipline, up-to-date weapons all combined to build up a strong fighting machine. Louis himself supervised the choice of uniforms and equipment. Nicknamed 'The Great Victualler', he revolutionised methods of supplying an army, setting up dumps of food and fodder for the horses and inventing a portable oven so that bread could be baked while on the march. He supervised military plans and preparations with a real sporting passion. In 1672 he was preparing to turn his attention to the Dutch, whom he referred to as 'a collection of maggots governed by businessmen and cheese merchants.' With England and Sweden, Holland had formed a Triple Alliance 'to curb the ambitions of France'. Holland was a republic, the people had dared to revolt against a king. Holland had personally insulted Louis in her newspapers. Holland was a Protestant country, Catholics were not allowed to hold any office of importance. Holland imposed heavy tariffs on French wine and brandy. Holland was to be taught a lesson; and Louis, encouraged by Louvois, again prepared for war. England and several German princes allowed themselves to be bribed into supporting France, and on 6 April 1672 Louis's army of 100,000 swept northwards. On 12 June it crossed the Rhine. True, the river was only four feet deep at that point, but to Louis it was a bold stroke for France and *La Gloire*, that bright phantasm which beckoned him as the vision of the Radiant Orb did Nelson. In Paris a triumphal arch, the Porte St-Denis, was erected, and poets wrote eulogies comparing Louis to Caesar.

In the face of invasion the Dutch breached the dykes. Within five days an area of two hundred square miles around Amsterdam was flooded to a depth of four feet. Farms, crops and animals, country houses with their beautiful gardens and their valuable tulip collections, vanished beneath the water. It was a kind of national suicide, but it stopped the French in their tracks.

Louis returned to Paris in a hurry in order to control the international situation more effectively. He hoped that with the coming of winter the flooded Dutch lands would be frozen over, and the French cavalry could lead an attack on Amsterdam; but the weather remained unusually mild, and time slipped away, destroying Louis's chances of a swift victory. Spain, Austria, Denmark and several German states entered the war in support of Holland in 1673, and Charles II of England made a separate peace with the Dutch. France's great general Turenne was killed in battle against German troops in Alsace, Condé retired because of ill health. Increased taxation to pay for the war led to revolts in the French provinces. Louis had failed to subdue Holland, but under the Treaty of Nijmegen in 1678 France retained Franche Comté and several fortresses along a strip of territory two hundred miles long which stretched from Dunkirk to the Meuse and gave her a stronger northern frontier. His main prize from the Dutch war, though, was his reputation, his military glory. France's navy had been triumphant in the Mediterranean; she now owned Maastricht, Ghent, Ypres, Franche Comté and half of Flanders. The long war had made Louis, in his own view, master of Europe.

While the King's attentions had been engaged on military matters there had been drama among the ladies back in Paris. Madame, the beautiful Henriette, had been packed off to England in 1670 to negotiate with her brother Charles II, pledging him French subsidy in return for his signature on the secret Treaty of Dover. She was away for two weeks. After a joyful reunion and grief-stricken parting from Charles, she returned with the treaty and her brother's signature, to be fêted by the entire Court, with the exception of her husband and his homosexual cronies. Monsieur took her back to their château at St Cloud on 24 June, where at the end of the month she was suddenly struck down with acute abdominal cramps. As the Court stood weeping round the bedside of the dying woman, Madame whispered to the Queen that she feared she had been poisoned. Physicians quickly prepared antidotes, but to no avail.

Louis ordered a post-mortem examination which did not prove that she had been deliberately poisoned. Although her brother Charles II refused to accept that she might have died from natural causes, Louis preferred not to believe that his brother might have murdered his own wife. The mystery has never been finally solved.

A year after Henriette's death, as soon as the appropriate time for Court mourning had passed, Monsieur married for the second time. Princess Elisabeth-Charlotte of Bavaria, known as Liselotte, was a large blonde German girl with a love of outdoor life and a broad sense of humour. Hefty, hale and hearty, Liselotte's country-wench appearance appalled the dainty, affected Monsieur and the rest of the Court, accustomed to the airs and graces of the fashionable beauties of the day. Liselotte's chief pleasures were hunting and letter-writing, and it is from her letters, funny, malicious and often ribald, that we get a vivid picture of life at Versailles. She found it difficult to take the French nobility serious-ly, despising their artificial way of life, their man-ners and their morals. She was not greatly impressed with her new husband, comparing his looks un-favourably with those of the King. 'Never were two brothers more dissimilar,' she writes, adding that they were in fact very fond of one another. Monsieur's girlish looks had faded. He was dark and swarthy, with eyes like blackcurrants, a large nose and a mouth, filled with ugly teeth, that was too small. Monsieur, in turn, despaired of his rebellious buxom lady and her inelegant appearance. He tried to encourage her to dress fashionably, even offering to apply makeup with his own hands. After one such attempt she declined further attempts to convert her from a German tomboy to a French exquisite.

Monsieur, though a homosexual, was compelled to fulfil his marital obligations, however distasteful he found the heterosexual act. He managed well enough to bring about the births of three children, after which this ill-matched couple led quite separ-ate lives, though as good friends, genuinely fond of one another. Madame never took a lover, but she worshipped the King, who treated her with a brotherly affection. In spite of being one of history's most noted homosexuals, Monsieur had two wives, an official mistress and several legitimate children, of whom four survived to adulthood. Every Roman Catholic royal family has Philippe d'Orléans among its ancestors. He was aptly remembered as the Grandfather of Europe.

Louise de La Vallière had been planning for some time to retire into a convent. Since a mysterious ill-ness in 1671 she had become more and more attract-ed to a religious life. She wished, as Mme de Sévigné related, 'to be allowed to dedicate the rest of her life to her salvation - having devoted all her youth to the King.' At one stage she removed herself to the Convent of Sainte-Marie de Chaillot, but the King followed her and persuaded her to return to Court. But Louise had suffered enough insults and indignities, even being expected to act as godmother to the children de Montespan bore the King each year, and eventually, in 1673, Bishop Bossuet persuaded the King to allow his ex-mistress to become a nun.

Louise bade the Queen farewell, begging her forgiveness, dined with Louis and Mme de Montespan, and the next day entered the convent which was to be her home for the next thirty-six years. The King wept at her departure, though it was said he would never forgive her for preferring another to himself, even though that other was God.

Invitations for the ceremony at which Sister Louise de La Miséricorde took her final vows were greatly sought after. The King's mistress became a Bride of Christ, and in one of the most austere of orders her lifestyle was to be very different. Mme de Scudéry, commenting on the ceremony in a letter to Comte de Bussy, says, 'She never looked more beautiful or more content. She should be happy if only because she no longer has to lace up Mme de Montespan's stays. If the truth be told she was a real martyr...'

High Noon

1674 – 1680

THE MOST SUCCESSFUL YEARS of Louis XIV's reign coincided with the reign of Mme de Montespan over his heart. Her highly cultivated literary and artistic tastes influenced the cultural development of the era. Her personal friends included Racine, Molière, Boileau and La Fontaine, and it was on her recommendation that Louis appointed the Florentine musician Lully as director of the Royal Opera. Athénaïs shared the King's passion for architecture and landscape design, and with the construction of Versailles well under way she ensured that her own apartments there would be superior to the Queen's.

Marie Thérèse was to regret the departure of Louise de La Vallière. Though she had resented the King's first official mistress, the tactful Louise had always been respectful and considerate towards her lover's wife, unlike the haughty Mme de Montespan, who considered her position as King's favourite to be superior to the Queen. The Duc de Saint-Simon says, 'Mme de Montespan's court became the centre of Court, the source of all pleasure, of all fortune - the hope and terror of ministers and generals... It was likewise a shame and disgrace to all France.'

For a long time the Queen had been in ignorance of Louis's involvement with Athénaïs. Louis had insisted on La Vallière's remaining at Court for the simple reason that it would draw attention away from his new favourite. When Athénaïs's marital problems had been resolved, and La Vallière been allowed to leave the centre of the stage, Athénaïs could inherit the title of official mistress. The gentle Louise had loved the King as a man and for himself alone; Athénaïs loved him for his position and power. She became greedy and demanding; she asked for presents of money and jewellery, her pearls had to be larger than the Queen's. The Queen's train was carried by a mere page - Athénaïs had a duchess to carry hers. She drank too much, she was fond of her food, she gambled for high stakes. She was witty and amusing, but the rest of the Court were wary of her quick and frequently acid tongue, taking care not to pass under her windows when the King was with her; they called it 'passing through heavy fire', an expression that was to become a popular catch-phrase at Court.

Athénaïs gathered her family around her and arranged for them to receive especial favours from the King, ensuring that they all attained positions of power. Begging Louis for a country house for herself, she spurned the plans for the first, considering it fit only for a common actress. Her château at Clagny, which took ten years to build, was modelled on the Palace of Versailles.

It was inevitable that the Queen would eventually find out about the relationship between her husband and Athénaïs. 'She had loved Mme de Montespan,' the Marquise de Caylus says, 'because she had believed her to be a respectable woman, loyal to her duties and to her husband. Thus Her Majesty's surprise equalled her sorrow when she later found her to be unlike what she had imagined.' The Queen's own frequently-heard comment was, 'That whore will be the death of me.'

In 1674 the de Montespan marriage came to an end with a judicial separation, officially because of the Marquis's 'profligacy in financial matters' and physical cruelty. He had custody of the two children of their union, but Athénaïs showed little interest in them, remarking unemotionally that she hoped their father would ensure that their education would be of a standard consistent with their rank and station.

Until the departure of Louise de La Vallière and
the legal separation of the de Montespans, the births
of the first four children born to Athénaïs and the
King were kept secret, the babies being hastily removed from their mother the moment they were
born and put in the care of a series of nurses. Athénaïs
appeared singularly unmoved at having to part with
her babies; there were more important things in her
life than maternal indulgence. (Six of the seven
children she bore to the King were physically defec-
tive. Three died in childhood, and of the others only
the Comte de Toulouse was completely normal.)

The separation made it possible for Louis to acknowledge the Royal Bastards, whom he legitimised.
It also enabled the birth of the fifth baby to be greeted openly. The task of removing the first four babies
at birth in conditions of great secrecy, placing them
with nurses and supervising their foster homes, had
been given to an old acquaintance of Athénaïs, Mme
Scarron, a widow in her early thirties. Sensible, reli-
able and the soul of discretion, she and her late husband, the witty versifier Paul Scarron, had in their
younger days been the centre of an intellectual circle,
holding a salon where they received the most brilliant and famous people in France. Now existing on a
small pension and living in a Paris convent, Françoise
Scarron was a tower of strength to her friends,
always available when help was needed. When
Athénaïs proposed engaging the services of this
worthy lady the King was not in favour. He disapproved of Mme Scarron and her intellectual
friends, and was left in little doubt that she
thoroughly disapproved of him. Athénaïs was insis-
tent, though, and Mme Scarron needed the money.

Having accepted the care of the King's bastards
with some misgivings, Mme Scarron conducted her
difficult duties with her usual diplomacy and effici-
ency. Talking to the girls of St Cyr, the famous girls'
school she founded many years later, Françoise
Scarron told them about her early days as governess
of the royal children.

This rather strange honour gave me infinite
trouble and cares. I would climb ladders to do the

upholsterer's work and hang curtains because they could not be admitted to the houses. The wet-nurses would not lift a finger for fear of tiring themselves and spoiling their milk. I would often go from one to another, on foot, in disguise, carrying clean linen or meat under my arm and sometimes, if one of the children was ill, I would spend the night there, in a little house outside Paris. In the morning I would return home by the back door and after dressing, enter a coach at the front door, to drive to the Hotel d'Albret or de Richelieu, in order that my social circle should not suspect that I had a secret to keep.

In 1671 the children, domestic staff and nurses were set up in a house on the rue de Vaugiraud, a large and handsome house set in extensive gardens. Mme Scarron, with the title of governess, was installed in charge of this household and here the King, always a loving and devoted father, came to visit his family.

Having officially recognised the existence of his children by Athénaïs, Louis now wanted them with him under his own roof, and in 1674 the family moved to Saint-Germain. Athénaïs was not enamoured of the idea. The maternal rôle had never appealed to her, and she was becoming increasingly irritated at the amount of time Louis spent in the company of the children and their governess. She had no cause for jealousy. The King had come to admire and respect the prim little woman who carried out her duties so devotedly, but it was inconceivable that he felt any romantic interest in this deeply religious person who made no secret of her disapproval of the adulterous relationship of the children's parents.

In 1675 the King awarded the discreet Mme Scarron a large sum of money in gratitude for her devoted care of his children. She bought the estate of Maintenon, ten miles from Versailles, and the King then addressed her as Madame de Maintenon. He later re-created the marquisate of Maintenon in her favour.

Athénaïs was in her prime at the age of thirty-eight, though childbearing and over-indulgence at the table had caused her to put on a lot of weight. Dieting and perfumed massages for two to three hours each day helped to combat the problem, but the King's eye was beginning to rove again. Now in his late thirties, Louis's sexual appetite seemed stronger than ever. Dutifully sleeping from time to time with his wife and spending at least an hour a day in his mistress's boudoir, he nevertheless embarked upon a series of affaires with other women. 'All the Court beauties,' wrote Mme de Sévigné, 'are on the alert to see which way the King will turn.'

'They lay seige to the heart of a Prince as to a citadel,' Louis himself protested as he accepted the favour of one lady after another. Athénaïs raged and sulked, her mood swinging from sullen depression to feverish gaiety. The Queen had resigned herself to Louis's infidelities, but Athénaïs could not accept them. Feeling her attraction for him was weakening, she was determined to go to any lengths to preserve her position as favourite, consulting fortune-tellers and even resorting to having love philtres concocted to slip into his food, a practice she was to regret later.

Upon the scene in 1679 came a very young and very beautiful girl. At seventeen, Marie Angélique de Fontanges arrived at Court and fell violently in love with the King, encouraged by her parents, who let it be known that she had been destined since her early youth to attain this illustrious position. 'An extraordinary blonde beauty, the like of which has not been seen at Versailles in many a year,' reported one ambassador. 'A form, a daring, an air to astonish and charm even that gallant and sophisticated court.' Mme de Caylus, putting a feminine point of view, says that 'Her head was empty except for romantic notions inspired by her provincial education and by the panegyrics on her beauty. The King in truth was attracted solely by her face.'

The King was intoxicated with the beauty of his new young mistress. It did not matter that she was 'as stupid as a basket' (his own words), as he found intellectual stimulation in the company of Mme de Maintenon, often spending two or three hours in the afternoon in her apartment 'chatting to her with such friendliness and intimacy that her position is the most enviable in the world' according to Mme de Sévigné. Athénaïs, consumed with jealous rage, swept out of Court in a fury, taking all her possessions and her entire retinue with her; the final straw had been the elevation of Mlle de Fontanges to the rank of duchess, a title Mme de Montespan could never aspire to, her official but absent husband being a mere marquis.

In January 1681 Marie Angélique gave birth to a stillborn child, and was never to recover completely. The King's intolerance of anyone who was sick or depressed caused him to fall out of love rapidly, and the wilting favourite was taken to a convent, where she soon died of pneumonia. Louis did finally visit her reluctantly, and managed to produce a few emotional tears at the death bed. Marie Angélique's last words, received with some scepticism by the Court, were 'Having seen tears in the eyes of my King I can die happy.'

Again, as in the case of the first Madame, poison was suspected, and though an autopsy insisted upon by Mlle de Fontanges's family attributed her death to natural causes, no one really believed it. It was whispered that Mme de Montespan was guilty, but no one dared voice their suspicions in the King's hearing. Athénaïs was back at Court, quarrelling violently with Mme de Maintenon, whose deepening friendship with the King she considered might be more than platonic. Louis tried to keep the peace between them, at one point declaring in exasperation 'It is easier to make peace in Europe than between two women.' Athénaïs, finding that her overblown beauty no longer had the power to inflame Louis's desires, resorted again to dabblings in black magic. It had been a source of wonderment how she had kept Louis physically enslaved for so long. His fits of dizziness, lassitude and the recurring headaches which he complained of were assumed to be caused by his excessive sexual activities, but it was now to be revealed that she had for years been giving him aphrodisiacs.

In January 1680 the Paris police arrested a number of people accused of poisoning. Olympe de Soissons, Mme d'Alluye and Mme de Polignac were accused of attempting to buy poisons in order to rid themselves of their husbands, but instead of facing the publicity of an enquiry the three women fled from Paris, their flight being taken as an admission of guilt. The chief among the accused persons was Catherine Monvoisin, La Voisin as she was known. She was a fortune-teller who would provide her clients with love philtres and occasionally with poisons to rid them of unwanted husbands. It transpired that she also performed abortions and celebrated Black Masses, sacrificing human babies to the Devil. After she had been found guilty and burnt at the stake her daughter gave evidence and claimed that Mme de Montespan had been one of her mother's regular clients. It was confirmed by others that Athénaïs had bought aphrodisiacs from La Voisin to give to the King secretly, and later poisons with which to kill Louis and Mlle de Fontanges. She had also had Black Masses to the Devil celebrated over her naked body by a defrocked priest, a ceremony which involved the sacrifice of a new-born baby.

By the King's command such accusations were concluded by the Court to be lies on the part of the accused persons trying to defame the King's mistress. The whole affair was hushed up and the papers containing the evidence against Athénaïs were given to the King in person. He burned them with his own hands. She was probably innocent of the gravest charges, but guilty of experimenting with love potions. At any rate, although he never believed in the guilt of the woman he had loved for twelve years, Louis could no longer trust her. She was allowed to continue living at Court and he continued to see her regularly and give her presents, but he was a changed man. Amorous adventures appealed to him no longer; he spent more and more time in the comforting presence of Mme de Maintenon.

Versailles:
and an Uncrowned Queen

1680 – 1683

VOLTAIRE DESCRIBED VERSAILLES as a 'great caravanserai filled with human discomfort and misery', but on the surface it was grand, glorious, unique. Those whose ambition was to live in its fairy-tale surroundings were prepared to put up with the disadvantages.

After Fouquet's imprisonment in 1661 Louis had appointed the three men who had created the magnificent estate at Vaux-le-Vicomte for the discredited superintendent of finances to design and build Versailles - le Nôtre, le Brun and Mansart. Colbert had hoped that the King would settle in Paris, rebuild the Louvre Palace and redesign and develop the capital. 'Nothing can add a greater glory to princes than buildings,' he wrote in a letter to Louis. 'All posterity will judge them by those great mansions which they have constructed in their lifetime.' He was determined that the administration, the economy and the arts should be directed from the capital, and that Paris should be worthy of such an exalted position. The city had improved beyond recognition since Henry IV had established a framework of plans and building regulations, but the elegance of the new churches and fine private houses, the beauty of the newly designed Tuileries gardens, and the creation of the Cours de la Reine could not hide the disadvantages of a city housing a massive population of 450,000. Congested traffic caused continual delays and the *boue*, a mixture of mud and sewage, made the streets unsightly, unhealthy and dangerous.

Louis disliked Paris for the memories it held for him. The most unhappy years of his childhood had been spent there during the *Fronde*, and in any case he loved the countryside and open spaces. Hunting was his favourite sport, next to which he enjoyed walking or riding in the forests with his close friends. Initially Versailles was to be a country residence where he could hold his fabulous parties and entertainments for his latest favourite, but Louis was more and more drawn to the place, and determined that it should outshine Vaux-le-Vicomte.

It seemed to everyone except the King that Versailles was just about the most undesirable spot in which to create the masterpiece that he visualised. Saint Simon wrote: 'Versailles, that most dismal and thankless of spots without views, woods or water, without soil even, for all the surrounding land is quicksand and bog, and the air cannot be healthy.' Louis took no notice of anything anyone said; he had his Grand Design in his head. Le Nôtre drew up plans for the new gardens, and work began as fields were ploughed and hundreds of great trees were brought from all over the country and re-planted to create instant forests, just as Fouquet had had done, but on a much grander scale. The vast formal gardens were planted with lawns and flower beds. Paths and avenues led into bosky groves, temples and statues stood at every corner. Three thousand orange trees were planted in ornamental pots, four million tulip bulbs were imported from Holland. There was a collection of exotic animals housed in a small zoo. Water was carried four miles from the Seine by means of an extraordinary machine with 223 pumps and fourteen hydraulic wheels, supplying 1,400 fountains. All the ponds and streams were drained in order to supply more water. The poisonous air round the marshes killed off hundreds of labourers. Mme de Sévigné wrote, 'Every night wagons-full of the dead are carried out... The melancholy processions are kept secret as far as possible in order not to alarm the other workmen.'

The King made frequent visits to see how the

work was progressing. His open-air 'green rooms' were constantly being added to so that he could hold even more elaborate parties. The new town of Versailles was laid out by Le Nôtre, and land was given to people of wealth and rank who were allowed to build houses conforming to an approved specification.

Jules Hardouin Mansart was the chief architect, agreeing to design the palace only if he were given a free hand to do exactly as he pleased. He designed it in the grand classical manner based on Greek and Roman temples, giving the impression of magnificence and majesty. Around the original hunting lodge were grouped pavilions and long wings of pale stone with columns, pilasters and high façades facing a great cobbled courtyard. In the park Louis built other smaller palaces - the Trianon, 'a palace of marble, jasper and porphyry' for his ladies, and his own personal home, the beautiful house of Marly, 'a sumptuous and delightful abode'.

Inside the palace the decoration was directed by Charles le Brun. Now given a chance to show his genius as a decorator on the grand scale, this brilliant painter produced huge religious and mythological pictures for the walls and ceilings; he brought in sculptors from all over France to reproduce the royal features on statues personifying Greek gods, while goddesses designed in classic poses were given the faces of the King's mistresses. As director of the Royal factory at Gobelins, Le Brun collected the most proficient and gifted craftsmen in the land to carry out his designs. Tapestry makers, weavers, dyers and embroiderers, goldsmiths, cabinet makers and engravers - there were specialists in every conceivable art or craft of decoration producing masterpieces of furniture, carpets, decorations, everything needed to turn the palace of Versailles into a showcase for French artists and craftsmen. In a Golden Age of French culture, Louis XIV was himself the leading patron of the Arts; painters, writers and musicians all had some connection with the Court, many receiving pensions from the King or finding themselves noble patronage.

On 6 May 1682 the Sun King and his Court moved into Versailles. Louis announced that from that date Versailles would be his official residence and seat of government. Far-flung members of the French aristocracy left their estates in the provinces and flocked to Court. The élite of society, the rich, beautiful, clever, the arrogant, stupid, corrupt-anyone permitted to live in the privileged circle moved into Versailles - if they were lucky, perhaps to a couple of dark airless attic rooms. Those less fortunate had to find lodgings in the town. Estates were left to deteriorate while their masters, living in the artificial world of the Court, squandered their money on a life of pomp and splendour, flaunting their fine clothes and jewels, strutting about 'embracing and congratulating those who receive favours' and whiling away their lives gambling and indulging in love affaires. 'The Court does not make a man happy,' said La Bruyère, 'it prevents him from being happy elsewhere... it is hard to accustom oneself to a life that takes place in a waiting room, in courtyards or on a staircase.'

Life at Court was a continuous theatrical performance. The King's every action was part of an elaborate ceremonial; his day scarcely varied from the time he was woken at eight o'clock by the musicians playing outside his window. The *grand lever*, his rising ceremony, was conducted by specially chosen courtiers and favoured members of his family. There was fierce competition for such honours as handling the royal shirt or holding the royal candle. It was the King's deliberate policy to stimulate and encourage this rivalry, for when the nobles spent their lives in plotting for small distinctions they had little time to spare for political intrigue.

Louis's day ended with a similar ceremony, his *coucher*, when he undressed in public with the same formalities as he had dressed in the morning. Between the *lever* and the *coucher* the King's day was filled with ceaseless activity. Mass in his chapel, long regular working hours with his Council, hunting in the forests, walking in the parks, visits to his mistresses, huge meals eaten in public, every day culminating with a series of entertainments, fêtes in the gardens in the summer, ballets, concerts, dances throughout the year. Louis's sister-in-law Liselotte describes a typical evening in a letter:

> Every Monday and Friday is *jour d'appartement*.
> All the gentlemen of the Court assemble in the
> King's antechamber, and the women meet in the
> Queen's rooms at 6 o'clock. Then everyone goes in
> procession to the drawing-room. Next to it there is
> a large room, where fiddles play for those who
> want to dance. Then comes the King's throne-
> room, with every kind of music, both played and
> sung. Next door in the bedchamber there are three
> card-tables, one for the King, one for the Queen
> and one for Monsieur. Next comes a large room -
> it could be called a hall - with more than twenty
> tables covered in green velvet with golden fringes,
> where all sorts of games can be played. Then there
> is the great antechamber where the King's billiard
> table stands, and then a room with four long tables
> with refreshments, all kinds of things, fruit tarts,
> sweetmeats, it looks just like the Christmas spread
> at home. Four more tables, just as long, are set out
> in the adjoining room, laden with decanters and
> glasses and every kind of wine and liqueur. People
> stand while they are eating and drinking in the last
> two rooms, and then go to the rooms with the
> tables and disperse to play. It is unbelievable how
> many games there are: lansquenet, backgammon,
> piquet, reversi, ombre, chess, Trou Madame,
> Berlan, summa summarum, everything you can
> think of. If the King or Queen comes into the room,
> nobody has to rise. Those who don't play, like
> myself and many others, wander from room to
> room, now to the music, now to the gamblers -
> you are allowed to go wherever you like. This goes
> on from six to ten, and is what is called *Jour
> d'appartement*. If I could describe the splendour
> with which all these rooms are furnished, and the
> amount of silver there is everywhere, I should go
> on for ever. It really is worth seeing.

Mme de Maintenon was secure in her position as
King's favourite. Confidante, friend and adviser
she surely was, but lover she was not. Wedded at
the age of sixteen to the crippled Paul Scarron, who

was unable to consummate the marriage in the normal way, Françoise had been subjected to a series of sexual indignities by her late husband which had caused a lifelong repugnance to any physical relationship. Many years later, when lecturing the schoolgirls at St Cyr, she told them that wives were 'obliged to accept every whim and every strange kind of behaviour on the part of their husbands... it would be difficult to foretell to what lengths they might go.' Françoise was a handsome woman who did not lack for suitors at Court, but her life was dedicated to bringing up the King's children. She could not approve of his generally dissolute way of life, and was one of the few people at Court who longed for a simple lifestyle away from the formality, intrigue and excesses of Versailles.

Until the end of 1679 her position was that of governess to the King's illegitimate children, but they were now growing up and a new post has to be found for her. The Dauphin was eighteen, shortly to be married to a German princess, Marie-Anne Victoire, daughter of the Elector of Bavaria, and Françoise was made second lady of the bedchamber to the new Dauphine. The king spent more and more time in her apartments, where they would pass quiet evenings in conversation, occasionally joined by the Dauphine. Louis's devotion to Françoise was apparent to everyone; though the relationship remained platonic she dominated him emotionally and spritually. He could hardly bear her to be out of his sight. No longer did the ladies of the Court vie for his favours; he showed no interest in any of them. His excessive sexual appetite seemed to have abated, perhaps because he was no longer being topped up with aphrodisiacs by the out-of-favour Mme de Montespan.

He seemed content to renounce the sins of the flesh and become a model husband to his neglected Queen, urged on by Mme de Maintenon. The King at that time, wrote Mlle d'Aumale, showed his wife attentions and affections to which she had not been used and which made her happier than she had ever been; she was touched to tears, and said in a kind of transport of delight, 'God created Mme de Maintenon in order to give me back the King's heart.'

Marie Thérèse was delighted with her beautiful apartments at Versailles; she blossomed in her new-found happiness and became quite animated. Everyone at Court knew the King was sleeping with her as she always went to Communion the next day. She liked to be teased about it and 'upon such occasions used to laugh and wink and rub her little hands.' She presented Mme de Maintenon with a portrait of herself framed in diamonds as a token of gratitude.

The Queen's happiness lasted for two years. In the summer of 1683 she developed an abscess under her left arm. Though in a great deal of pain she was blissfully happy, declaring that a fête given her by the King had been the most enjoyable she had ever known. Three days later she was dead from blood-poisoning caused by the appalling medical treatment. As she lay dying she took the ring from her finger and handed it to Mme de Maintenon with the words, 'Adieu, my very dear marquise; to you I confide the happiness of the King.'

'Poor woman,' said Louis of his dead wife. 'This is the only time she has ever given me any trouble.'

He recovered quickly from his grief. Françoise de Maintenon was given rooms in the Queen's suite, and soon, probably in the autumn of 1683, she and Louis were secretly married. It was a morganatic marriage. Mme de Maintenon did not become Queen, but kept her own name and her own liveries. Louis referred to her simply as 'Madame'.

For more than thirty years Françoise de Maintenon remained the uncrowned Queen of France. The King remained in love with her for the rest of his life, but she was popular with few other people. Her influence grew as she gained confidence. Politics, religion, public and private morals she tackled remorselessly 'with eyes still lowered, the modesty of a nun and the authority of a moralist.'

Sun in Eclipse

1683 – 1714

'THE KING IS BEGINNING to think seriously of his salvation,' wrote Mme de Maintenon hopefully. 'If God preserve his life there will soon be only one religion in his kingdom.'

Louis's marriage to Françoise de Maintenon had a profound effect on his personality. His faith, learned from his mother, was simple and unquestioning. He hated heretics who did not accept the Catholic faith, but he opposed the authority of the Pope over the French Church as he considered that he himself was the only ruler of France - a ruler appointed by God. Henry VIII had thought much the same thing. 'Kings depend upon God and recognise no power above them,' Louis said. He was forced to realise, however, that he needed the Pope's support to put down religious disagreement among his subjects.

France had been experiencing a religious revival; as new monasteries and convents were established, monks and nuns abandoned the worldly lives they had been leading and gave themselves to prayer and austerity. The Jesuits established schools and colleges in France and became influential as confessors and preachers at Court. The order of Sisters of Charity worked among the poor, and the Congregation of the Priests of the Mission was founded to help and educate village clergymen. The most famous of orders was the Order of Visitation, which consisted of nuns who were allowed to leave their convents and care for the sick.

There were movements in the French Church which aroused Louis XIV's opposition. One was Quietism, which taught that the higest aim a believer should set himself in his religious life was to gain through prayer and meditation an immediate personal knowledge and experience of God, and this could be done without the assistance of the services, sacraments and clergy of the Church. The Quietists were unpopular with the Catholic Church, which saw that the danger of such beliefs was that they made the Church unnecessary.

The religious sect of Jansenists believed that man was so sinful that he could not save his soul except through God's grace. They felt that the Catholics were morally lax because they allowed people to sin, provided they confessed, were absolved and took communion. Their strict morality did not appeal to Louis, who preferred his Catholic belief that man's soul was not endangered just because he enjoyed worldly pleasures.

Influenced by Mme de Maintenon, Louis's piety became excessive and misdirected, and, determined to ensure that France would be wholly Catholic, he turned against the Huguenots. He agreed with Bossuet's motto, 'one king, one law, one faith', and believed the Huguenots' existence was a political danger to his rule. Of the twenty million people in France about two million were Protestant. It did not appear an insurmountable task to the King and his Catholic advisers to persuade them to renounce their faith when convinced by 'preaching and persuasion'. Jealous of the Huguenots' success as tradesmen and merchants, Louis systematically attacked them to make them change their faith. They were banned from holding public offices or entering professions; missionaries preached the advantages of conversion to Catholicism, with the added inducement of tax relief for those who complied. Huguenot schools were closed and churches destroyed. French dragoons returning from the wars were billeted in Huguenot homes and encouraged to bully and torture the families.

By the autumn of 1685 the Huguenots had been reduced by three-quarters. Many had become

Catholics, and a quarter of a million of the most intelligent and highly-skilled had emigrated to Germany, Holland and England. Louis now decided to revoke the Edict of Nantes, by which his grandfather Henry IV had recognised Protestantism, guaranteeing the Huguenots religious freedom. This caused a vast exodus; those who could of the remaining Huguenots fled the country, though they knew that if they were caught they would be executed or sent to the galleys. Over 400,000 inhabitants were lost to France by Louis's persecution; merchants, craftsmen, doctors, lawyers and bankers. The navy lost nine thousand sailors, and nearly thirteen hundred soldiers and officers fled, leaving France's defences depleted. She also lost the foreign craftsmen and workers brought into the country by Colbert, many of whom were Protestants.

Liselotte's letters expressed the feelings of many of the King's critics:

> The old whore (Mme de Maintenon) and Père de Lachaise (Louis's confessor) convinced the King that all the sins he had committed with Mme de Montespan would be forgiven if he banished the Protestants, and therein lay the road to heaven. This the poor King firmly believed, and that is how the persecution of the Protestants began.

'My realm is being purged of bad and troublesome subjects' announced Louis. But he had revoked the Edict of Nantes not as an act of piety but to increase his own glory, to offer a wholly Catholic France to God, and to be remembered for it.

Louis XIV's army was the largest in the world since the days of the Roman Empire, and with it he waged war almost continuously for fifty years. Europe became alarmed at the growing strength of France and a king at the height of his power, now known as Louis the Great. The revocation of the Edict of Nantes aroused Protestant indignation, and England and Holland were alarmed by the expansion of France's overseas trade and the growth of her navy. Louis's continued use of his military power to spread through Europe was seen as an increasing danger, and in 1686 Spain, Holland, Austria, Sweden and several German states formed the League of Augsburg. When William of Orange, Louis's greatest and most hated rival, became King of England, France was alone against Europe and England was drawn into the Alliance.

Louis was not discouraged by the opposition of the other European countries. In 1688 he invaded Western Germany, seizing Cologne and the Palatinate. He had hoped that a short limited war would disrupt the League of Augsburg, but this time his resort to military action did not get him what he wanted. The Allies decided to act; the War of the League of Augsburg began and continued until 1697, spreading through Flanders and Italy and even as far as the American Colonies. Within two years the English and Dutch navies had defeated the French navy at Cape La Hogue and France no longer had any chance of achieving naval supremacy.

The brutal tactics of Louis's army horrified Europe. As the soldiers advanced across the Palatinate they destroyed the whole area so that the German armies could not follow. Houses, castles and whole towns were wrecked and people killed or forced to leave their homes. Vineyards and crops were burned and bridges destroyed. Louis, supporting the dethroned James II of England who had fled to France, sent troops and a fleet with James to Ireland, where at the battle of the river Boyne they were defeated by William of Orange. In Holland the French advance was halted by the rivers and waterways which provided Holland's allies with strong lines of defence.

As the war dragged on the enormous financial drain on France proved too great and Louis had to agree to peace. The Treaty of Ryswick in 1697 meant that though he was left with Alsace and Lorraine, he had lost virtually all the other territory France had gained. He was forced to support William of Orange as King of England.

Since 1691 Louis had been his own Minister of War; he directed the Siege of Namur in person, and until 1693 served as commander in the field. A great firework display at Versailles celebrated his military achievements, though the French people may well have disagreed with their King's opinion of his triumphs. 'Louis XIV gives peace to Europe' was the theme of the display.

Peace for France was not to last. In 1700 the sickly Charles II of Spain died, and the Spanish crown was offered to Louis's seventeen-year-old grandson, Philippe, Duc d'Anjou, who had been named as heir in Charles II's will. If Louis accepted the Spanish crown on Philippe's behalf it was inevitable that Spain would then be under French domination, a fact that would not be likely to be accepted by Austria or by England. On the other hand, if he declined the offer of the Spanish throne it would be offered to the Hapsburgs, who would have the support of England and Holland. Louis accepted and thus made war inevitable. He made a disastrous pronouncement to the effect that his grandson, though King of Spain, would still be able to inherit the throne of France; then he seized the 'barrier fortresses' in the Netherlands, claiming them in the name of Spain. On James II's death, though bound by the Treaty of Ryswick to recognise William of Orange as King of England, Scotland and Ireland, Louis insisted on recognising James II's son as the true King. Everyone at Versailles felt he had gone too far. A correspondent from Court wrote:

> Everybody here expects a terrible war to break out next spring, and preparations are already being made for this eventuality. So now the kingdom is going to be ruined once again, before it has had time even to make good the ravages of the last war. I think we are going to pay dearly for this crown of Spain which the King has bought for his grandson at our expense. It will cost us a fortune to prevent it being snatched away from him. Frankly, we are great fools to ruin ourselves for the aggrandisement of others.

Europe had had enough of Louis XIV and his *gloire*. In 1701 the European powers united in the Grand Alliance, and war again swept across Europe, the War of the Spanish Succession. Louis had no great generals now in the mould of Condé and Turenne; his army was depleted from past wars, and France no longer had the finances to rebuild it to its former scale. France lost her place as military leader of Europe at the battle of Blenheim in 1704, when she tried to force her way into Germany. John Churchill, Duke of Marlborough, led the English against her, killing or scattering 30,000 of the French army of 50,000. In Spain the new young King Philip V was threatened by an Imperial army led by the Archduke Charles, who also claimed the Spanish throne. Spain was in danger of falling until the Imperial army was halted by a French victory at Almanza in 1707. In the meantime England captured Gibraltar, opening the Mediterranean to her navy. English ships sailed the Mediterranean 'like swans on the river at Chantilly'.

A total eclipse of the sun was an ominous portent on 11 May 1706, as Marlborough defeated Villeroi at Ramillies, a defeat followed by others in October. France was in economic and financial chaos. Louis sent his gold plate to the Mint, encouraging the princes and nobles to follow his example so that enough money could be raised to pay the army whose morale was desperately low, soldiers and officers having to sell weapons and clothes in order not to starve.

In January 1709 the Seine froze over in the worst winter France had experienced for over a century. Trees and vineyards were ruined, half France's live-stock froze to death and the mortality rate doubled in Paris - even members of the Court at Versailles died from the effects of the cold. Soldiers were frozen to death at their posts and citizens of Paris dropped dead in the streets. As a result of the floods which followed, the crops were rotted in the ground. 'The earth seems dead,' wrote Fénelon, the former tutor to the Duc de Bourgogne; 'it promises neither fruit nor harvest.' Now that the people of France were dying from famine, Louis was shocked into realising he would have to confront the Grand Alliance and beg for peace.

The terms offered by the Allies were unacceptable, particularly the demand that Louis should hand over Spain to the Archduke Charles, to do which he would have had to declare war on his own grandson. 'Since war there has to be,' he declared, 'I prefer to wage it against my enemies than my children.'

There were more defeats for the French as Marlborough triumphed at Oudenarde in 1708. At dawn on 11 September 1709 Marlborough and Prince Eugéne attacked the French army near Malplaquet. Eleven thousand Frenchmen died, the army was decimated and Louis, his *gloire* tarnished and with personal tragedies to bear at home, became subject to severe fits of depression.

Marlborough's plan had been to capture 'barrier fortresses' on the Franco-Dutch borders and then possibly invade France itself; but because of a change in the English Government and the English desire to end the war, peace preliminaries were signed by the French and English. Vendôme beat the Imperial troops in Spain, and Villars recovered most of the lost French territories in Flanders. Louis was now in a favourable position to negotiate and on 11 April 1713 the peace of Utrecht was signed.

In 1714 Louis was forced to acknowledge George of Hanover as successor to William of Orange, and though Philip V was allowed to remain King of Spain he had to give up his claim to the French crown. England won large parts of Canada from France, and Gibraltar and Minorca from Spain. The Netherlands, Naples, Milan and Sardinia were claimed by the Hapsburgs.

With the throne of Spain safe for Philip, Louis had won what he set out to achieve, but at a terrible cost. France was virtually bankrupt, her people's morale was low. Louis XIV's sun was setting.

The Sun Sets

1709 – 1715

LOUIS WAS GROWING OLD, and France was a depressed country suffering from the aftermath of expensive wars which had imposed a terrible financial burden on her people. Taxation fell most heavily on the peasants, who were already dying of hunger and disease due to continual bad harvests. Unemployment in the towns caused many people to go to Holland, Italy and Spain in order to find work, and the streets of France were thronged with peasants, former soldiers and labourers, now reduced to begging. At least a tenth of the population had become beggars, scratching in the gutters for scraps at a time when a loaf of bread cost as much as a labourer's daily wage.

During the nightmare winter of 1709 there was a hunger-march to Versailles from Paris, and for the first time since the *Frondes* Louis heard the shouting of the mob. 'The common people are dying like flies,' wrote Mme de Maintenon. There was criticism of Louis's rule from the Church, for its encouragement of persecution and indifference to the people's sufferings. Bishop Fénelon advised the King, 'Your loyal subjects are dying of hunger... You are praised to the skies for having impoverished France and you have built your throne on the ruin of all the classes in the state.'

Louis's confidence in divine sanction and his own kingly duty remained supreme. In the midst of defeat and discontent he stood unshaken, though Mme de Maintenon was to record that he was subject to fits of uncontrollable weeping when in the privacy of their apartments. There were personal sorrows within the family, too, as the royal physicians helped to hasten the demise of relatives young and old with the practices of bleeding and purging which they employed for the mildest of ailments, and which weakened the patient and lowered his resistance. Mme de Maintenon convinced the King that these national and family misfortunes were a punishment by God to teach him humility and ensure his salvation.

Life at Court had lost its sparkle. The nobility deserted Versailles and moved to Paris where they built their own houses. Life was altogether quieter, money was short, even for them, and they had lost their taste for extravagant entertainment. Louis became one of the soberest men in the kingdom. He abandoned his magnificent costumes; the dazzling prince of former years was now a stout figure dressed always in a plain brown coat, his bald head covered by a short wig instead of the flowing curls he had always favoured. He still enjoyed remarkably good health as he entered his seventies, though his face was sunken as a result of a dental operation which accidentally removed part of his jawbone. In 1686 he had had a successful though agonising operation for an anal fistula, but otherwise his passion for physical exercise and his careful though somewhat excessive diet seemed to have saved him from serious illness.

Françoise de Maintenon, three years his senior, also enjoyed good health, though permanently racked with rheumatism which she blamed on Louis's passion for fresh air. She wrote to the Bishop of Chartres about Louis's sexual appetite, which she considered should have declined somewhat as he reached his seventies. 'Surely twice a day is excessive?' she asked. The bishop replied that she should be grateful that it was in her power to keep His Majesty from sin. She was to think of Heaven, where the subjections of the present life would be over.

When away from the King, Françoise de Maintenon's life revolved around the girls' school she had founded at St Cyr, a little village near Versailles. Three hundred girls were carefully chosen on the grounds of their breeding and family connections to be given a good education and trained to take their place in the outside world. The King showed a great interest in the school, insisting that the uniforms should be pretty and feminine and that there were to be no unnecessary rules and not too much 'holiness'. 'There are plenty of good nuns in the world,' said he, 'and not enough good mothers.'

Even so, not all the girls complied with Mme de Maintenon's ideals of plain living and study, and she found it necessary to deliver regular lectures to them in an effort to raise the tone of the school. She deplored their use of cosmetics, and even more worrying was their behaviour towards each other. Liselotte records:

> Some of the young ladies there had fallen in love with one another; they were caught committing all sort of indecencies. Mme de M is supposed to have cried her eyes out. She had all the holy relics put on display to drive out the devils of lechery. Also she had sent for a priest to preach against lewdness, but he talked about such hideous things that none of the modest ladies could bear to listen; they all left the church, but the culprits were overcome by uncontrollable giggling.

Mme de Brinon, the Superior, had herself become full of her own importance, daring to challenge Mme de Maintenon's authority. She was removed from her post, and Mme de Maintenon decided to change the school's policy and turn it into the typical convent she had once visualised if the King had not interfered with her plans. The teachers were forced to take the veil. There were to be long periods of silence, more housework, and no more literature lessons or poetry reading. The pupils were appalled. The King sent his band to play outside their windows to cheer them up, but despite this kindly gesture the girls became increasingly bored and depressed. They were to find an outlet for emotional expression when Mme Guyon, a disciple of Quietism, joined the school and encouraged them to share her brand of religious fervour. Mme de Maintenon also came under her influence for a short time, but the Church renounced Quietism, Mme Guyon was imprisoned in the Bastille for eight years, and Louis was so displeased with his wife's involvement that he barely spoke to her for two weeks. The school at St Cyr became a convent of a particularly severe Order, and the majority of the girls eventually became nuns. Mme de Maintenon spent a great deal of her time there, in the one place where she felt at peace and to which she would retire after her husband's death.

Monsieur, the Dauphin, the King's only living child by Marie Thérèse (his only legitimate child, in fact) was a dutiful son, plump, amiable but dreadfully dull. His wife, equally plain and dull, bore him three sons who were more like their grandfather the King in temperament, intelligent, handsome and strong-willed, a source of joy to their elders. Also at Court were the five surviving children of the King's former mistresses. They spent much of their time squabbling among themselves and getting into trouble, so that Louis was constantly having to keep the peace between them and rescue them from the consequences of their misdeeds.

The happiest time in the King's later years was when his brother's grand-daughter, Marie Adéläide of Savoy, came to live at Court in 1686 when she was ten years old. She was the grand-daughter of his brother Philippe and his first wife, Henriette-Anne of England. She was therefore partly a Stuart, which is very apparent from a portrait of her in hunting dress. Perhaps her arrival brought back memories of the dead Minette to Louis. With her all formality fled. He treated her like a beloved daughter, petted and spoiled her, or would have done if her peculiarly sweet nature had not protected her. At twelve years old she was married to her cousin the Duc de Bourgogne, the Dauphin's eldest son, though they did not live together until she was fourteen. As she matured she became more sober and level-headed, but she was delicate and most of her babies were to be stillborn. The Duc was quiet and hardworking. Louis had great hopes of his future, admitting him to his Council when the boy was hardly out of his teens.

The Dauphin was fifty-three in 1711 when he suddenly fell ill with smallpox. Though he seemed to be making a good recovery, his condition suddenly worsened and he died, leaving the Duc de Bourgogne the new heir to the throne. The new Dauphin was handsome, intelligent, hardworking and kindly. Louis's spirits began to rise, now that he could pin his hopes on this excellent young man and his enchanting wife, Marie-Adélaïde, and their two small sons, the Duc de Bretagne and the Duc d'Anjou. Such a royal family could only bring happiness and prosperity to France.

It was on 19 January 1712 that the Dauphin received a warning from Spain to himself and his wife to beware of poison. Marie-Adélaïde was a little worried by it; she had been told she would not live to be twenty-seven. She was unwell, but only from toothache and early pregnancy. Some days later she took a pinch of snuff from a box given to her by the Duc de Noailles; it was Spanish snuff. When the box was searched for later it had vanished, never to reappear.

Symptoms of illness set in which were taken for measles. Nine doctors took over, on which her condition rapidly worsened. On 9 February she died. A few days later her husband, who was also ill, declined sharply. He knew that he was dying, and he was glad, because without Marie-Adélaïde life was not worth living. 'I die with joy,' he said. The bodies of husband and wife were taken together for burial at Saint-Denis. On 8 March their elder son, the Duc de Bretagne, was bled for the measles rash he and his brother had developed. He struggled and raved, crying out that he didn't want to make the horrible journey to Saint-Denis. But the doctors made sure that he went there. He was the third Dauphin of France to die in eleven months.

The old King was distraught, broken with grief. Those he loved were dying all around him, and the heir to his throne was a sickly toddler, who, though the only one of his family to recover from the measles, seemed unlikely to survive for long. In fact he grew up to be exceptionally robust. The Dauphin's youngest son, the Duc de Berry, was hastily groomed to take his brother's place on the throne of France should the little Dauphin die, but two years later he was fatally injured in a hunting accident.

Louis XIV was a defeated man; moody and silent, his health started to deteriorate. His appetite was fading, and it was noticed that he would fall asleep during entertainments. His once magnificent physique crumbled; he became a shrivelled little grey old man. In foreign capitals bets were placed that he would not last the year. In August 1715 he complained of pains in his leg. Sciatica was diagnosed, but the leg got more and more painful until at the end of the month black spots developed and it became obvious that they were gangrenous.

Louis knew he was dying. He spent his final days making sure his affairs were in order and saying his farewells to his family. The Dauphin, now a healthy five-year old, was brought to his bedside. His grandfather virtually handed his kingdom over to the child, much as his own dying father had done when he was a year younger than the present Dauphin.

> You are going to be a great King. Do not copy me in my love of building or in my love of warfare. Try to live peacefully with your neighbours. Remember your duty and your obligations to God; see that your subjects honour Him. Take good advice and follow it; try to improve the lot of your people, as I, unfortunately, have never been able to do.

He kissed the child and blessed him, adding, 'I depart, France remains.' From now on it was noticed that he spoke of the little boy as King and of himself as already gone.

Françoise de Maintenon had scarcely left the King's room in the past days. Now, worn out and distressed, she made her farewells to her husband. 'I had always heard it is difficult to die, but I find it so easy,' he told her. They would soon be united, he assured her. As he lapsed into unconsciousness she was advised to leave, and went to St Cyr where she was to spend the next four years until her death at the age of eighty-four.

On 1 September 1715, aged seventy-seven, Louis XIV died after a reign of seventy-two years, the longest in European history. The glory of the Sun King had long since faded; the people who had once loved and venerated him now blamed him for the sorry state of the nation. As his body was taken to the Basilica of Saint-Denis it was escorted by a brawling drunken mob. Though still some eighty years in the future, the scene for the French Revolution had already been set.

Louis XIV

1638 – 1715

Louis XIII (1601-1643).

Anne of Austria, (1601-1666), daughter of Philip III of Spain.

Louis XIV and the Queen Regent. On the right is his younger brother Philippe, Duc d'Anjou.

Louis XIV as a child, a portrait by Mignard.

Cardinal Mazarin (1602-1661).

Mazarin with the young Louis, an engraving depicting the education of the boy King by the statesman.

Louis XIV's first visit to his *Parlement*, 18 May 1643. 'Gentlemen, I have come to express my affection and goodwill towards my *Parlement*. My Chancellor will give you my wishes.'

Gaston d'Orléans (1608-1660), the rebellious uncle of the King.

Louis XIV in 1648, aged 10.

Cardinal Richelieu (1585-1642). An etching by C.O. Murray after Philippe de Champaigne's famous triple portrait. Richelieu was largely responsible for Mazarin's rise to power and for creating the circumstances which eventually led to the absolute power of the Monarchy.

The 'Mazarinettes', Olympe, Hortense and Marie.

The King makes his triumphant
way through Paris, after four years
of bitterness of the *Fronde*.

Louis II, Prince de Condé (1621-1686).

The King in July 1658 convalescing after a fever.

1659. The young King in all the splendour of his majesty.

The marriage of Louis XIV to Maria Teresa, daughter of King Philip IV of Spain, June 1660.

Louis XIV c.1660, at about the time of his marriage. Painting by Mignard.

Anne of Austria, mother of Louis XIV.

Louise de la Vallière (1644-1710), the King's official mistress.

Philippe, Duc d'Orléans (1640-1701), the King's younger brother ('Monsieur').

Louis XIV inspects the Gobelin Tapestry Works which contributed so much to the visual arts of his reign. His visit is commemorated in this tapestry of astonishing opulence.

Nicholas Fouquet (1615-1680). Superintendent of Finances until 1661 when Louis had him arrested and imprisoned.

Jean-Baptiste Colbert (1619-1683), who succeeded Fouquet after his arrest.

Fontainebleau.

Louis and his Court outside Arras.

'The nobleman is the spider and the peasant is the fly'.

Peasant life was hard as this contemporary print shows, with women doing much of the hard labouring on the land.

Life on the land (note the tax collector).

Athénaïs de Montespan (1641-1707). She replaced Louise de la Vallière as the King's mistress in 1667.

Versailles. Work had begun in 1661 to transform a hunting-lodge into a palace.

The founding of the *Academie des Sciences et des Beaux Arts*, 1666.

Charles Le Brun (1619-1690), architect and painter, and Pierre Mignard (1610-1695), the painter.

André Le Nôtre (1613-1700). Landscape gardener and architect, responsible for designing the gardens of Versailles.

Louis as a young man painted by Le Brun.

LE VRAI PORTRAIT DE LA VOISIN.

The notorious La Voisin (1640-1680). She was at the centre of the fearful poisoning scandals at Court.

Louise de la Vallière, after she had been replaced as the King's mistress and had entered a convent.

'Monsieur' on horseback in fancy dress as King of Persia.

Bishop Bossuet (1627-1704). He persuaded the King to permit Louise to enter the convent.

Louis declaring war on the Dutch in 1672.

Bernini's great equestrian statue of Louis XIV at Versailles.

'*An Assembly of Gods and Goddesses*', by Nocret. Louis is depicted as Apollo and Monsieur, his brother, as Pluto. His mother is Cybele, the Mother of the Gods, and the Queen is Juno.

Louis XIV,
Commander-in-Chief of
the Army.

Statue of Louis XIV.

Molière (Jean-Baptiste Poquelin), (1622-1673).

Jean Racine
(1639- 1699).

Pierre Corneille
(1606- 1684).

Jean de La Bruyère
(1645-1696).

Jean de la Fontaine
(1621-1695).

Louis XIV was a great patron
of the Arts. His reign
inspired a vast legacy of
enduring literature and
drama. Here seen dining with
Molière at the Comédie-
Français.

The *Grand Lever*.

The King and his courtiers at
Versailles.

Louis playing billiards.

Madame de Maintenon (1635-
1719). Secretly married to Louis in
1683 after the death of Marie Thérèse.

Louis in May 1701.

Paul Scarron, former
husband of Françoise de
Maintenon, who died in
1660.

Versailles, 1722.

Louis at the capture of Mons, 8 April 1691.

Defeat for the French fleet at La Hogue in May 1692.

Contemporary cartoon of the 'War of the
Spanish Succession', 1701. It ridicules the
French for their vanity.

Madame de Maintenon
with the young
daughters of noble
families in the school she
established at St Cyr,
where she retired after
the King's death.

Versailles.

Louis XIV and his heirs. Left to right:
Duc de Bretagne (with his governess, Duchesse de Ventadeur), the
Grand Dauphin, Duc de Bourgogne.

Louis XIV on his deathbed. He died on 1 September 1715, aged seventy-seven, after a reign of seventy-two years, the longest in European history.

Epitaph from the King's tomb.

ICY EST LE CORPS DE LOUIS ·14·PAR
LA GRACE DE DIEU ROY DE FRANCE
ET DE NAVARRE TRÈS CHRESTIEN;
DECEDÉ EN SON CHASTEAU DE
VERSAILLES LE PREMIER JOUR DE
SEPTEMBRE ·1715·
REQUIESCAT IN PACE

A contemporary engraving of the Lying in State at Saint-Denis, 9 September 1715.